THE TRIAL OF ROGER STONE

THE TRIAL OF ROGER STONE

MILO YIANNOPOULOS
DANGEROUS BOOKS

THE TRIAL OF ROGER STONE

Milo Yiannopoulos

First edition, 2020

Cover Design: Milo Yiannopoulos
Original Artwork: C. Mitchell
Photography: Mike Allen

Published by Dangerous Books

ISBN: 978-952-7303-59-7

To John:
Marriage to you
is never a trial.

"IT'S RARE THAT I'M ACCUSED OF SOMETHING I'M NOT GUILTY OF."
— ROGER STONE

CONTENTS

INTRODUCTION: STONE'S RULES

"It's my understanding that Mr. Stone has brought his own sketch artist to court with him today," said Judge Amy Berman Jackson, reproachfully, before ordering the young woman in question to leave the room. If you know a little about Roger Stone already, this story will sound plausible to you—perhaps even likely. *Of course he did.* That's so on brand! Especially for a man who's said to have once remarked: "I'm photosensitive. I'm sensitive when people don't take photos."

There was just one problem. It never happened. The judge was mistaken. The truth of this sketch-artist skirmish was much less eyebrow-raising than the Twitter commotion suggested: A female artist sympathetic to Stone showed up on the first day of trial, without his knowledge. The court's own security guard let her sit in the little reserved bullpen in front of the normal gallery, alongside the court-appointed artist. One of the judge's rotund, beady-eyed bevy of female clerks noticed, reported it to Judge Jackson, and—hey, presto!—another thread of Stone mythology was woven into the public record, with no hope of future correction.

This fake story, spread endlessly by gossipy reporters covering the case, made Stone look as though he wasn't taking his criminal trial seriously. That can have serious consequences to a man facing jail time, or entreating the judge for an appeals bond—especially, as we will see, when the judge in question is one of the most ferociously partisan members of the federal judiciary. Basically, when you're dealing with an enemy who will take any tweet, any joke, any remark, any meme... *anything*, and, if at all possible, contort and repackage and misrepresent it as a threat, or a "lie," or evidence of "witness tampering"... well, a history of sassy remarks and a natural inclination toward showmanship and performance art can be a liability.

As a former senior editor for *Breitbart*, a *New York Times*-bestselling author and an international political celebrity and free speech icon, I've heard my share of so-called conspiracy theories. I've heard conservatives talk endlessly about double standards and unfair treatment. I've listened as Republicans have complained about how they're regarded versus their Democrat peers. Most of the time, the conservatives are right. Almost all of the things they claim are true! Wait long enough and the things you hear on conservative talk radio generally prove to be pretty much spot-on. These revelations have come thick and fast in the past half-decade, because the

Trump presidency has exposed collusion, cronyism and entrenched bureaucracies in the federal government at a scale that has stunned most Americans.

But never in my life have I sat in a courtroom and watched a put-up job unfold before my very eyes, and experienced a chill creeping down my spine as I slowly come to realize the terrifying power of a team of government lawyers determined to take someone down, whether they committed a crime or not, and how the full might of the American jurisprudential system kneels to accommodate them.

In November 2019, Roger Stone was found guilty of one count of obstruction—that is, of lying to Congress during an investigation—five counts of making a false statement to the government, and one count of tampering with a witness. Of all these charges, the last is the most preposterous. But none of them should ever have been brought against him.

This book is about getting justice for some of the people this abusive, overweening and institutionally Left-leaning federal government apparatus has hurt, especially since this President was elected. It's about a broken and illegitimate Special Counsel system that will haunt and handicap every President until it is overhauled. And, finally, it's about what the current incumbent of the Oval Office, Donald J. Trump, can and must do to make things right and unravel a horrible injustice.

But first, let me tell you about the hero of our story. Roger Stone is sixty-seven, though he does not look it. He is one of those older men who has somehow maintained an athletic build well into his more advanced years. His hair is bleached white, or sometimes a sort of cream, depending on the salon and Stone's mood. You will never catch him with roots: He is far too well-maintained for that. He understands that appearances are, if not everything, then at least most of the time enough, which is why he owns a hundred tailor-made suits in a variety of styles, most of which you would nonetheless describe as "Mafioso opulence."

He sports a year-round tan, which he considers an essential part of his self-presentation, and has, I would say, two primary modes of facial expression. One is kind and faintly amused—this is uncle Roger leaning in to his natural charm, a sort of airy nonchalance of the type the Italians have perfected. The other is a distinctive downward smile that is really more of a snarl—and this what people mean when they talk about the dangerous political operative Roger Stone. This snarl-smile has the effect of drawing attention to his very slightly pointed ears, and gives him the impression of a mongoose about to bite the head off a snake, which is as good a description of Stone's political career as I can think of.

To the odious, monotonously-uniformed army of Washington, D.C. insiders and swamp creatures, you would say that Roger is pretentious and silly, and indeed people with no imagination or love of style describe themselves as quickly bored by his affectations. But the funny thing about Roger Stone is that his style is so much more sincere than theirs is. He shows us who he is. The unvarying sartorial drabness of D.C. is really a kind of camouflage: Underneath the sameness hide intrigue, plotting, and a surreal degree of amorality. Roger, on the other hand, is who he says he is, and he is how he dresses, and this feels real, and it is perhaps the true, atavistic reason they hate him so much: He allows himself authenticity.

One of the many parts Stone plays on our T.V. screens is that of court jester or Holy Fool: the colorful truth-teller in the middle of it all, who dances playfully for the amusement of the crowd, but in whose jokes the plain truth resides while all around him are dodging the question. In literature, the jester is often the only one telling the truth at Court—and the only one with a direct connection to the audience. Stone eschews the false solemnity and social mores of the D.C. elites, recognizing them as a mask worn by the truly malevolent. As we will discover, Roger the Joker is the only one who tells the truth from start to finish—the Fool keeps his oath, as all around him are breaking their word.

It is an irony that Stone, famous for being well-dressed to the point of artifice, is the only person in our saga who shows true moral gravity. Why might this be? Because he is surrounded by an establishment that lies every day to preserve its power and maintain its prestige, even as the citizenry become ever-more cognizant of who they really are.

Twenty-first century American public life, in which everything depends on a person's connections and their ability to say the right thing in the right say, is an unconscious reconstruction of a royal court—a place in which everyone is distantly orbiting power, desperate for a taste of it and doing anything necessary to stay in favor. An elaborate system of manners more tiresome and ever-changing even than Versailles under Louis XIV keeps everyone lying and looking over their shoulders, perpetually terrified of the easy misstep that will kill their careers. The joke of it all is that they are circling a mirage, for there is no King, only the People—and the People have had enough of them.

In such a broken place, it takes a Fool's courage to tell the truth about the corruption, to stick to his word, and to stand by his friends.

Roger Stone can pull off almost any item of clothing, but he has a set of apophthegms by which he lives, works and dresses, his style inextricable from his morality, called *Stone's Rules*, which is also the title of a book that collects all these maxims together. Some of them are original, some borrowed. Together they paint a clear picture of a man ruthlessly severe about a few core values—the proper way to break a trouser leg on a dress shoe, how to respond to an attack in the media—but resplendently libertine in the most enjoyable areas of life. *Stone's Rules* is most instructive when you observe the kind of things about which Stone does not have hard and fast rules: Sex, drugs and other pleasures, but also matters of culture, race and religion.

The man I know lives these values perfectly, breathtaking in his audacity and daring when it comes to clobbering an electoral opponent, iconoclastic about the causes he chooses to champion, depressingly strict about his tailoring, relaxed about other people's lifestyle choices, brutal in his foul-mouthed tirades, and, perhaps above all and despite the foregoing, uncompromisingly morally consistent in his Christian generosity to other human beings.

Despite his sophisticated tastes, Stone talks like a street-fighter. An eff-bomb is never very far away, usually sandwiched between a name-drop and a witty remark. Among his favorite axioms: "Admit nothing, deny everything, launch counterattack." "It's better to be infamous than never to be famous at all." "There is nothing worse than seeing ankle or a hairy calf when a man in a suit or trousers sits down." "Politics with me isn't theater. It's performance art. Sometimes for its own sake." "Stone's Rules exist because sometimes the truth is too painful, and the lies will land you in prison." And my favorite: "I never owned a pair of blue jeans until I met my second wife."

It is tough to get to know Stone just by seeing him on camera in his pomp, and impossible merely by reading reporting about him. It's unusual to meet someone successful who sincerely cares about the art of living as much as his day job. But you get an idea of this relentlessly, sometimes exhaustingly distinctive worldview when you learn that he has dedicated large portions of his life to drug decriminalization, animal welfare, serious head injuries sustained by N.F.L. players and, of course, driving Democratic politicians to panic and ruin. And even that doesn't tell the full story, because Stone once advised Al Sharpton, in the 2004 Democratic primaries.

In short, Stone is one of the last surviving radical individualists in politics, an arena that desperately needs original thinkers.

This book is the product of dozens of interviews—except with Stone himself, who declined to be interviewed or to speak about the case at all, as did his lawyers—and thousands of pages of publicly-available court transcripts, jury questionnaires and other documents, in addition to emails, text messages and conversations shared only with this author. It's also the result of two weeks of first-hand reporting from Stone's trial and sentencing in Washington, D.C.

Roger Stone knew the stakes when he decided to enter politics, and especially when he decided to play the game in the most aggressive way he could. No one escapes decades in the political arena without garnering a few scars—especially the men most anxious to go bare-knuckle. There are those who would say that this trial for petty nothings was a preordained and perhaps even fitting end—the inevitable nemesis after hubris—for a man who became rich and famous tormenting his political adversaries with wicked, manufactured trivia. Indeed, it can be hard to muster sympathy for a man so self-consciously larger than life, a man who owned four Jaguars and showed up to parties in bespoke suits and silk slippers paid for by third-world dictators.

And yet, knowing all this, but also knowing the Roger Stone the rest of the world has not met—the compassionate, generous, animal-loving, dope-smoking avuncular hero of my political genesis—I am stupefied by the scale of injustice visited upon him in that Washington, D.C. courtroom, and by the scope and reach of the corruption that enabled it.

You, reading this book, may have no time nor empathy nor especially warm feelings about Roger Stone. But his story matters, because it has revealed things about American jurisprudence that every citizen must know, and about which every American citizen should rightly feel incensed. I know it's easy to assume the worst, or most ridiculous, version of events where people like Roger Stone are concerned. As a political provocateur and polemical columnist I've experienced the same phenomenon.

We bring it on ourselves with our brazenness and flamboyance and occasional cruelty and our generally reckless attitude to life, don't we? Sometimes it can seem as though we don't take anything seriously at all. I can hear my mother's voice as in my head as I write this. *You can't call yourself a "mischievous provocateur" or a "dirty trickster" with a straight face, or revel in similar names given to you, all the while mocking and needling and humiliating your enemies, and then cry foul when someone hurls a rotten egg back.*

Okay mom, but, well, three things. Firstly, this was not a rotten egg. It was a thermonuclear bomb.

Second, there are some double standards at play here. In twenty-first century America, you are allowed to be funny and interesting and charismatic and *also* powerful and influential and intelligent and politically savvy... if you're a liberal. So Jon Stewart and Bill Maher are allowed to make jokes, and have their jokes granted as such, and they are also allowed to make serious points, and have those insights treated with respect. But conservatives don't get the same pass. It's assumed that if you're Right-wing, you must be either a clown or totally evil. So our jokes are shorn of context, stripped of all meaning and nuance and presented as serious commentary. And our sincere analyses are dismissed as trifling, or as insufficiently erudite or "intellectual" to be worthy of sober consideration.

Third, when a falsehood is spread by America's reckless and puerile mainstream press, ordinarily a person in the public eye can make efforts to correct the record. They can tweet about it. They can demand to have their response edited into online reporting. They can go on *The View* and trash their haters. But, because we were effective and high-profile supporters of President Trump, people like Roger Stone and I no longer have the same tools at their disposal as everyone else.

Like comedian Gavin McInnes, congressional candidate Laura Loomer and, yes, the present author, Stone has been a victim of Big Tech's targeted censorship campaigns, which were designed to knock out popular, influential dissident thinkers on the center-Right and ensure that the results of the 2016 election could never be repeated. We're on an unofficial but universally-observed mainstream media blacklist that ensures we're never invited to defend ourselves from fictitious allegations or even just express our opinions on unrelated matters about which we have experience and expertise.

By far the most damaging effect of social media de-platforming is that you can no longer set the record straight about anything. Journalists don't bother asking you for comment, and most of the time don't bother including anything you send them by way of rebuttal or clarification, because they know it doesn't matter. They just write what they want, knowing there will be no consequences. And they're right! No one is searching Gab or Telegram or Parler—a few of the alternative social networks of choice—when a story hits Twitter, Facebook and C.N.N. to see whether it's real or fake. The result? Almost everything you read about your favorite dissident conservatives in a newspaper, or hear about them on the T.V., is untrue. Eventually, even our supporters start believing things about us that are false—even if they sound pretty baller in retrospect, like bringing your own sketch artist to court with you.

That's the first reason I've written this book—to get Roger's story down correctly while it's fresh, before they deny any of it ever happened. For people like Roger and me, our reputations are shaped entirely by hostile political forces dedicated to our complete annihilation and ritual public humiliation. So as a Trump-supporting author, media figure or political celebrity, you do what you can, in whatever format you can, to get the truth out there, since you're constantly operating from deep within enemy territory.

Of course, it didn't help that the judge in this case committed the most egregious violation of an American citizen's First Amendment rights that I think I've ever seen, gagging Stone from speaking about the case in public or defending his reputation, thereby ensuring the narrative would be written entirely by his political enemies—and guaranteeing that the jury only heard that side of things, too.

But there's a second, more important motivation for me in writing this book. The American media did everything it could to turn Roger Stone's trial into something fundamentally unserious. They tried to suggest Stone wasn't treating it with the requisite level of respect, that he was aloof and unbothered—providing ammunition to an activist judge desperate for excuses to throw the book at a man she obviously loathed. And they went loco on conspiracy theories, like the one about Roger putting crosshairs over the Judge's face on Instagram. More about that later.

Throughout Roger's trial, there was feverish tweeting about what I and other famous supporters of Roger's were wearing, and who was lunching with whom. Reporters were thrilled to see colorful Trump-supporting celebrities in a courtroom, because it gave them the chance to distract readers from the injustice in front of them and trade in imaginative caricatures. I even saw a diary item on the C.B.S. News website about "rightwing firebrand Milo Yiannopoulos ... also there for a second day, sitting in the family's pew and taking notes in a cheetah-print notebook with gold-leafed pages."

There was, in fact, a solemn reason I traveled to Washington, D.C., for Stone's trial—a moral imperative—that went beyond our friendship. Other journalists, I knew, would focus on inflatable Trump balloons erected outside the courtroom by protesters, instead of engaging with the substance of the case in the fair-minded and attentive manner this case warranted. It turned out that I was correct. Almost no one mentioned how anemic the government's case was against Stone, or the glaring credibility problems with each of the witnesses. In their orgiastic frenzy of gloating, the press got just about everything wrong—including about my notebook.

It wasn't cheetah print. It was leopard.

Most of all, journalists forgot what the press is there to do—hold power to account. They forgot to ask why a trial was happening at all. They forgot to ask whether naked political vengeance is a sound basis for criminal charges. They forgot to ask who is served by handing Roger Stone an enhanced custodial sentence that might mean he will die in jail. And they forgot to ask whether the American taxpayer should keep picking up the tab for vicious, underhanded, ideologically-motivated attacks from disgruntled F.B.I. agents and Justice Department employees. They forgot, or preferred not to ask, about the extraordinary use of force in the paramilitary dawn raid on Roger's Florida home.

None of that suited the overall purpose of the press coverage, which was to suggest that Trump's presidency is illegitimate, and that the President is a crook, because lots of his longtime friends and aides are getting convicted. No one mentioned that these offenses— with perhaps one or two exceptions—were meaningless process crimes and procedural infractions, and none of them had anything to do with anything Special Counsel Robert Mueller's investigation had been set up to uncover, namely, that the Trump campaign had colluded with the Russian government.

Certainly, no one asked why a few rowdy text messages between Roger Stone and his erstwhile friend, a disheveled alcoholic radio host by the name of Randy Credico, were being cooked up into an absurd charge of "witness tampering" by a prosecutorial team desperate to save some face and rescue a conviction or two out of the smoldering ruins of the Mueller shambles.

Until Stone's sentencing, in February 2020, when a few brave souls like Fox News's Tucker Carlson and radio host Mark Levin started hitting the story hard, there was no one on the airwaves talking honestly about this vindictive prosecution, which is why so few Americans understand how Trump advisor and loyal friend Roger Stone came to find himself in such an awful position, and why he was convicted of lying to Congress despite the preposterously flimsy case against him. Even on *Fox*, you didn't really hear the full extent of how Stone was condemned to a Soviet-style trial until Carlson began his daily entreaties to President Trump in early 2020.

Astonishingly, no reporters from any mainstream news sources have investigated or explained how the judge in this case barred every powerful line of defense from Stone's legal team, and how the jury was meticulously stacked against Stone, and comprised entirely of Left-leaning Democrat voters, former Democrat White House employees and far-Left operatives and activists.

That is what this book will do. Some of the things you will read in these pages will astound you. Others will shake your confidence in the fairness and impartiality of the American legal system. Sorry! But these are things you need to know.

Underneath the social media flotsam, unremarked upon by C.B.S. and A.B.C. and cable news, and absent from the pages of *Politico* and *Buzzfeed*, was the true story of Roger Stone's trial—the one you haven't read until now. It is a story about injustice, about the state of our nation, and about corrupt and malicious government actors hell-bent on revenge because they still can't get over the 2016 election result. It's about one man's life destroyed because he wouldn't tell lies about an old friend. And it's about the outlandish, almost incomprehensible demands from federal prosecutors for a sentence of nine years for the offense of lying to Democrat Congressman Adam Schiff, an act almost no one in America believes should be a crime.

This story is about Roger Stone. But it's also about the wretched systemic failures and wretched people in the American intelligence, law enforcement and political establishments that some people collectively call the "deep state." I am still a birther, mostly because I am unaware of any "right-wing conspiracy theory" that is not eventually proven true. (And, you know, because Obama was probably born in Kenya.) But the deep state theory, initially scoffed at as fanciful by C.N.N., vindicated mere months later by the *New York Times*, has been revealed to us as a fact of objective reality as well as a persuasive explanation for many of America's chronic civil injustices and social wrongs, partly thanks to the trial of Roger Stone.

In what follows, I make no pretense to impartiality. Roger Stone has been a friend, a colleague, a fellow street-fighter and even a mentor to me. Since this debacle began, I have shed tears for him and for his family, who have been subjected to indignities and legal perversions too numerous to catalogue.

This is not earnest reportage, vainly grasping for illusory objectivity. It is not an academic work of history. It is something altogether more honest.

So far, the story of Roger Stone has been a strange and complex screenplay, written by the sort of people who always make conservatives the villains on T.V. This book will set the record straight. It is, in a manner of speaking, a morality tale—but one with more twists and deceptions, more disappointments and more astonishments, than any H.B.O. drama. In the course of this book, I will tell you what I know, and I will tell you what I saw, and I will not lie to you. That's all a writer can ever do. By the end of these pages, no matter your political orientation or opinion on the 2016 election or any of the major players in that drama, I hope you'll at least agree: What happened to Roger Stone was wrong.

Everyone loves a good courtroom drama, even though it can be difficult keeping abreast of all the characters sometimes. But you should pay attention to the details of this case for reasons that go beyond mere prurience—

or even *schadenfreude*, if you're a New York blogger hate-reading this introduction. Because there's a profound significance to Stone's story, which is that this is a rare instance in which the machinations of the deep state have been laid bare for the public to see. Ordinarily, these triangulations play out far from public view. So as you read about the trial of Roger Stone, I entreat you to consider the cruelty, brazenness and arrogance of the federal government, the judiciary and the media in this case, and ask yourself: If this is what they do in public, what on earth are they doing in private?

I can think of few stronger arguments than the Stone trial for reform of the way American citizens are governed and for the abolition or wholesale restructuring of failed institutions and practices, such as the Special Counsel, through which political actors in either party, and politically biased employees of the state, use taxpayer money to persecute their political opponents. Misuse of the justice system for political vengeance, no matter the direction in which firepower is directed, does not serve the American people. It does not further those noble goals upon which America's founding mythology rests. It helps no one and hurts everyone. Where we find it, we must expose and thereby exterminate it.

The perpetuation of Washington D.C. and all that Americans rightly hate about that place depends upon citizens not educating themselves. The bad guys rely on you ignoring the details. They rely on you getting bored and moving on to the next hot topic playing out on C.N.N. This is how the swamp functions: By constantly changing the story, hiding the details and misrepresenting even minor facts.

Like that one about the sketch artist.

The deep state thrives not only thanks to the opaque systems of protection they have built around their activities, but also by never standing still. There is always some fresh terror, and poorly-educated, inattentive citizens are doomed to chase the newest thing, like a kitten following a laser pointer, distracted from even the most sickening of scandals. That is why you should read this book. And why you should probably stop watching cable news.

Miscarriages of justice will go on so long as there is a justice system—an inevitable consequence of the fallibility and fallenness of Man. But where there are glaring invitations to abuse, we should act. America, having no King, is a country founded on Laws. Without the fair application of justice, the compact between the government and the governed no longer holds. I know people get bored hearing establishment Republicans bang on about the Constitution. I do, too. Like most people, I often want someone to come along and just fix everything for me. But for all their faults, the G.O.P. at least understands that the people are sovereign only insofar as they live by the Law. Without it, we are all tyrants to the extent our wealth, connections, education and malice allow.

Thanks to President Trump and even, in an enjoyable absurdity of our age, Kim Kardashian, progress is being made to correct the decades-long persecution of black Americans by the criminal justice system, a catastrophe set in motion by Bill Clinton's crime bill. Perhaps now it's time to look at some of the other ways in which the United States of America fails its people, and to seek not social justice, but true justice, an elusive but indispensable aspiration upon which the future of our country depends.

CHAPTER ONE:
IF HE DID IT

It had been a long time coming. But, finally, in 2015, Roger Stone saw decades of earnest plotting come to fruition. His old friend Donald J. Trump had bitten the bullet and agreed to run for President of the United States, confounding the commentariat, who reacted to his announcement with finger-pointing and derision. Stone was an official advisor to the campaign, and later told reporters that he'd been responsible for the "build the wall" policy.

It's impossible to figure out who, exactly, came up with that phrase, since Stone and Trump both habitually claim credit for everything that happens around them, but now that America has got to know Trump a little better, Stone likely has the better claim. In any case, he'd been planning this for a long time.

Although Roger Stone officially left Trump's campaign early on—Donald Trump can't stand anyone around him who gets as much attention as he does—it was only when Stone was let off the leash that he could really machinate for a Trump victory. Stone was on every T.V. channel and in every newspaper insisting that his man was not only a serious candidate, but the only man who could win. He became an omnipresent fixture on networks other conservatives shied away from, such as C.N.N. and M.S.N.B.C., as well as Fox News and the blossoming *InfoWars* empire.

When Stone published *The Clintons' War on Women*, a book two decades in the making, it killed Hillary's feminist credentials for good, and, together with Peter Schweizer's forensic bestseller *Clinton Cash*, helped to solidify the Clinton dynasty's reputation as corrupt, venal, morally reprehensible, hypocritical, untrustworthy and—crucially, since Democrats don't care about any of those things—*unlikeable*. With the narrative of Hillary's atrocious behavior toward Bill's rape and assault victims re-injected into the popular consciousness by Stone's book, there was enough name recognition of the likes of Juanita Broaddrick that Steve Bannon could daringly bring her and the other Clinton victims to a presidential debate, just to unnerve Hillary. With the exception of Trump's, "Only Rosie O'Donnell," it was probably the most delicious moment of the election.

When the miracle happened in November 2016, Stone wondered if he might finally get another coveted spot in a Republican President's inner circle, his first since Nixon, despite decades of continuous and wildly effective— if not always publicly acknowledged—operations for

G.O.P. candidates, such as the hand Stone had in the Brooks Brothers riots. These "riots" were really a minor scuffle, but they shut down a ballot recount in Miami-Dade and helped to hand George W. Bush the Oval Office. Stone had masterminded hundreds of political victories, and assisted several Presidents, but Trump was the first he could call a personal friend.

It wasn't to be. Almost immediately after the election, the impeachment drums began, the product of an enraged and bewildered Democrat Party's thirst for revenge. Intimates of Donald Trump, especially the more visible, unapologetic and colorful, were in the firing line.

We now know, thanks to an admission in the *New York Times*, that Roger Stone was spied on, almost certainly illegally, by the F.B.I. during the 2016 elections. The surveillance has never stopped, and continues to this day. For five years, federal law enforcement agencies have been snooping around in Roger's emails, bank records, social media accounts and mobile devices and eavesdropping on his phone calls. Sometimes this has been legal. Most of the time it hasn't.

Stone was quickly fingered as a target in the Mueller investigations, which failed to produce any evidence of collusion between the Trump campaign and Russia, but which snared Trump staffers and friends in a variety of meaningless process crimes, the product of thousands of hours of F.B.I. agent time trawling through private correspondence and personal data to assemble offenses wholly unrelated to the publicly-announced parameters of the Mueller report. When it became clear that the

3

Special Counsel was not going to lay a finger on Trump, it became all the more important to save face and make sure that half a dozen of Trump's friends and associates ended up in jail. So the screw was tightened around Stone, and a vindictive, politically-motivated prosecution for irrelevant, minor infractions—anything the feds could pin on him—was born.

Although the *New York Times* had revealed that Stone and others were being illegally surveilled, this fact is still denied by federal law enforcement officials, by members of the Special Counsel's prosecution team and even by the federal prosecutors who used the fruits of that surveillance in order to cook up charges to put Roger away.

Here's what they said Roger Stone did.

The Senate Intelligence Committee asked Roger Stone to preserve any documents he possessed related to Russian contacts. They asserted that Julian Assange's non-profit publisher of leaked documents WikiLeaks, and the Twitter account "Guccifer2.0," both of whom it was thought Stone was in regular contact with, were Russian assets. In WikiLeaks's case, this is an absurd and provable falsehood; in the case of Guccifer2.0, the jury is still out. What the Committee wanted to know was: What did Roger Stone know about WikiLeaks's drop of emails stolen from the Democratic National Committee, and when did he know it? The emails had helped Trump get elected, since they were released at the zenith of the 2016 campaign season.

If Stone was in touch with WikiLeaks, and WikiLeaks was really the Russians, and Stone was, in turn, also in touch with the Trump campaign, this might finally establish, however tenuously, a connection between Trump and Russia. Could this be the elusive smoking gun that would put Trump behind bars? The answer is obviously No, because the whole thing is piffle. But you can see why Democrats might have been excited about it.

From this moment on, there would be almost daily segments on C.N.N. and M.S.N.B.C. claiming Trump's arrest or indictment would be "coming soon," an ubiquitous ritual the media repeated for nearly two years. I know, I don't need to tell you. You remember.

In interviews, Stone artfully dodged questions about his direct contact, if any, with Julian Assange, while teasing interviewers with insinuations about an intermediary or go-between that he may or may not have had to WikiLeaks. In truth, he did have one: the sickly sometime comedian and Left-wing radio presenter Randy Credico, who had a close relationship with one of Assange's attorneys, and who had been contacted by several intelligence committees, as Stone had, to discuss the relationship between Stone and WikiLeaks.

Tortured by Californian bobblehead creep show Adam Schiff on an almost daily basis leading up to the launch of an official investigation, Stone maintained a vigorous schedule of interviews and cable news appearances. From C.N.N. to his own show on Alex Jones's *InfoWars* network, he fought back allegations made by Schiff, including claims that Stone realized could have only resulted from illegal leaks by dirty cops or intelligence surveillance.

Eventually, it became clear that Stone would be summoned before the House Select Committee on Intelligence. Stone moved first, offering to testify without a subpoena. But he wanted a public hearing, which Schiff and congressional Democrats refused to grant. That didn't stop Stone from releasing the testimony he gave before the committee, which you can find in Appendix II.

Contrary to the flood of fake news and assertions made by federal prosecutors later down the road, Stone remained in the hot seat for hours and answered every question, no matter how bonkers, about his alleged contact with Russian assets. After his spirited and defiant testimony Stone seemed to have the upper hand in the public square for a moment—so, naturally, that was the moment Twitter chose to suspend his account, purportedly for being mean to C.N.N. news personalities who were lying on a loop, based on no evidence at all, that "more indictments" could be announced in the "coming days."

Not much changed through the spring of 2018, as Stone got used to being in the cool kids' club of banned Twitter celebrities. (It gets better! I promise.) But, in March, one-time Trump aide Sam Nunberg began, inexplicably, to tell journalists that Stone had been in direct contact with Julian Assange. In a frantic, whistle-stop tour of T.V. stations—fueled by cocaine, according to a senior Republican strategist who shared a studio with him at the time—Nunberg claimed that Robert Mueller had "forced" him to spread this false story to media outlets.

The subpoenas began to fly. First up, Jason Sullivan, a social media consultant who worked with Stone for barely a month before being let go for producing nothing. Sullivan spent the next two years billing himself as Stone and Trump's social media consultant, a complete fabrication according to longtime Stone aide and journalist Jacob Engels. Sullivan agreed to interview with Mueller and comply with the grand jury request, and, it is believed, turned over information about Roger's Twitter account and social media activity that he had improperly gathered during his brief work tenure. Sullivan meekly acquiesced to any suggestion the Mueller team made.

Over the next several months, other Stone intimates, such as Manhattan Madam Kristin Davis, were also called in for questioning. Davis, who has a young child to whom Stone is godfather, said investigators were fixated on Stone's personal life and his relationship with the child, asking voyeuristic questions about Stone's sexual activities, and asking whether he was faithful to his wife. To put it mildly, their enquiries were not germane to the investigation and appeared to be designed to acquire blackmail material or other embarrassing evidence to later leverage against Stone. To her credit, Davis immediately went public about her creepy encounter with the feds.

Johnny Kakanis, a Florida resident who had worked as a driver and aide to Stone was brought in as well. Kakanis was questioned about Stone's finances. Henry "Enrique" Tarrio, Chairman of the men's fraternal organization the Proud Boys and a slightly tragic fixture of fringe Miami politics who dresses like a Cuban Abraham Lincoln, was subpoenaed and forced to testify. Tyler Whyte, the Florida State Chapter President of the Proud Boys was also dragged to D.C.

Jacob Engels, the young journalist who had enjoyed a close relationship with Stone for some seven years, was also summoned. Engels's boyfriend was harassed by federal agents hammering on their front door for days, before Engels returned from a business trip, only to be confronted by the F.B.I. while pulling weeds in the front yard.

2018 was to be the last year that Roger Stone would produce his annual, and nationally famous, *Best and Worst Dressed List*, a tradition he had continued for over a dozen years after the passing of fashion commentator Mr. Blackwell. The present author had the distinction of being listed in Best Dressed for several years in a row before ascending to the Hall of Fame in 2017, a testament to Stone's discerning judgment.

On December 3, 2018, President Trump tweeted: " 'I will never testify against Trump' This statement was recently by Roger Stone [*sic*], essentially stating that he will not be forced by a rogue and out of control prosecutor to make up lies and stories about 'President Trump' Nice to know some people still have guts."

When the *Guardian* optimistically collected together social media posts from lawyers who claimed that the Trump's tweet constituted "witness tampering," most observers laughed at the sheer silliness of the suggestion. But this shameless misrepresentation was a portent of what would come during Stone's trial, when boisterous macho teasing would be used to construct precisely the same charge.

* * *

Barely two months after Trump's tweet, immediately before dawn, the F.B.I. staged a televised raid on Roger Stone's home. Twenty-nine S.W.A.T.-uniformed agents stormed Stone's Fort Lauderdale residence, arriving in seventeen armored vehicles with K-9 units, helicopters and two amphibious units to march the white-haired sexagenarian, barefoot, from the premises. It was a staggering display of overkill.

Ordinarily, in non-violent cases involving high-profile people accused of political wrongdoing, a schedule is set with the accused's lawyers for an arraignment, and the defendant shows up to court as mutually agreed. Prosecutors knew that Stone was represented by counsel because they'd spoken to his lawyers less than forty-eight hours before the raid.

So there was no credible explanation for why a man of pensionable age with no criminal record and no history of violence, and who was not being charged with any violent crime, should have been subjected to this terrifying spectacle. Stone's wife, Nydia, is almost entirely deaf, and it's not outlandish to imagine some tragic accident triggered by panic thanks to this unnecessary thuggery. Fortunately, Stone had sensed the arrest coming, even though he did not know when or how, precisely, it would happen, and he answered the door in a t-shirt that read ROGER STONE DID NOTHING WRONG, as revealed by internal cameras on the Stone property.

The only plausible excuse for staging the *Blitzkrieg* on Coral Way was that Stone was a flight risk, and this is of course what federal prosecutors argued. Yet Stone possessed neither a firearm nor a valid passport on the morning he was arrested. To where could one of the most recognizable men in America possibly have fled with his Ralph Lauren-clad wife? In any case, this justification was exploded when, the very same day, the government itself did not oppose Stone being released on bail without so much as a cash bond.

And so we are left with the more likely explanation: That it was all theater, designed to damage Stone's image and make him look both guilty and dangerous to the public, thereby not only influencing public opinion, but also poisoning any future jury, who could not help but be affected by the shock-and-awe optics of the paramilitary raid.

By happy accident, C.N.N. was on site with the cameras rolling that morning. They caught the whole raid as it unfolded and broadcast it live to a rabid audience. I'm kidding, of course: It wasn't by accident. The timing and location of the camera crew was all pre-arranged with the F.B.I. Don't believe me? Consider the following: Roger Stone's street was sealed off by the F.B.I. hours before the raid to everyone *except* this C.N.N. camera crew, which Stone's home security footage shows setting up barely twenty-five feet from his front door a mere eleven minutes before agents arrived.

C.N.N. claimed its reporter just happened to be in the right place at the right time. Yeah, sure. There's only one plausible explanation, of course: The F.B.I. granted exclusive access to C.N.N. to film and broadcast the arrest. Oh, and just by the by, *a propos* of nothing: C.N.N.'s Josh Campbell, the first news correspondent to report on Stone's arrest, is the former special assistant to F.B.I. director James Comey.

I'm sure it's all just a gigantic coincidence.

Roger Stone's own lawyers first heard about the arrest from a C.N.N. producer calling for comment. A F.O.I.A. request from the transparency advocacy group Judicial Watch, asking for correspondence between C.N.N. and the F.B.I. in the days before the Stone raid, was denied without explanation. This is now the subject of a pending lawsuit.

Republican Senator Lindsey Graham has published a letter he wrote to the Department of Justice and the Bureau demanding to know who approved such a heavy-handed raid on Stone's home. To date, neither the F.B.I. nor the Justice Department has bothered to respond—at least not publicly. Special Counsel Robert Mueller has refused to comment on whether it was his office, the Bureau, or both.

Watching from home, you'd be right to smell a rat. Even the President realized something was off. "Who tipped C.N.N.?" tweeted Trump, right after Stone's arrest. Everyone was thinking it, including Stone's lawyers, who said they would ask at trial whether there was anything fishy about the "made for T.V." manner in which Stone was treated, since it suggested motives that go beyond the neutral application of justice and into partisan revenge and deliberate cruelty. Federal judge Amy Berman Jackson forbade the defense team from even bringing it up.

* * *

The terms Special Counsel and Independent Counsel didn't exist until after Watergate. Previously, the appointment was known as a Special Prosecutor. After Watergate, Independent, and later Special, Counsel was eased into use as a political public relations move. In fact, it was written into law, in 1983's reauthorization of the Ethics in Government Act, that Special Prosecutor, because it sounds a bit too harsh and confrontational, shall no longer be used in any official capacity, replaced ultimately today by Special Counsel.

But all three terms mean the exact same thing—a lawyer appointed to investigate and prosecute suspected wrongdoing where the usual authority may have a conflict of interest. Even that doesn't tell the full story. The concept comes from state law, in which courts, not politicians, were allowed to appoint Special Prosecutors when the usual attorney had been disqualified from a case because of illness, incapacitation, or proven, not suspected, conflicts of interest.

Today, the Special Counsel is something most Americans will never hear about outside of the federal level and presidential politics—when the President or a member of his administration is under investigation. The reasoning goes that the usual authority is compromised because he would be asked to investigate his boss, or one of his boss's appointees.

The first federal Special Prosecutor, John B. Henderson, was appointed by President Ulysses S. Grant, in 1875, to investigate the "Whiskey Ring" scandal, which involved whiskey distributors, I.R.S. agents and members of the Treasury Department siphoning off liquor tax revenues into political campaigns and their own pockets. Grant appointed a Special Prosecutor to avoid the appearance of a conflict of interest. Grant later sacked him for incompetence and hired a replacement—setting a precedent that Special Prosecutors can be both hired and fired by the President.

Presidents Garfield, Theodore Roosevelt, Calvin Coolidge, and Harry Truman all appointed Special Prosecutors to investigate scandals during their administrations, but not until the Nixon administration did this reach a constitutional crisis. Before being appointed Attorney General under Nixon, during Elliot Richardson's senate confirmation hearing, Richardson agreed to appoint a Special Prosecutor to investigate Watergate. Immediately upon taking office, he hired Archibald Cox.

Cox demanded the release of secret recordings Nixon had made in the Oval Office. Nixon refused, but the Court of Appeals demanded that he hand them over. Nixon demanded Cox be fired and instead of complying, his Attorney General resigned. He was eventually fired under the new Attorney General and Nixon dismantled the office of the Special Prosecutor. But after public outcry, he hired another. That Special Prosecutor, Leon Jaworski, continued Cox's work, demanding the tapes. We all know what happened after that.

The Special Prosecutor is an office in the executive branch. Nixon rightly argued questions about the separations of power under the U.S. Constitution. The Special Prosecutor answers to the President, who is the head of the executive branch, and the President cannot be forced to comply with a subpoena issued by his own subordinate.

Due to the Watergate constitutional crisis, in 1978, Congress passed the Ethics in Government Act, which established rules on Special Prosecutors. It basically said select members of Congress can request a Special Prosecutor formally to the Attorney General, but it's up to the A.G. whether to hire one. If he declines, he only needs to put into writing the reason.

The law was reauthorized by Congress four times, but it expired in 1999. Since 1978, about twenty Special Prosecutors have been appointed, but the law governing the process is no longer in effect. There is no federal law today governing the appointment of Special Prosecutors, but regulations established by Janet Reno, Attorney

General for most of the Clinton Administration, known as the Code of Federal Regulations, Title 28, part 600, remain in effect today in the Department of Justice.

These internal agency guidelines say that the Attorney General can fire a Special Prosecutor but he needs very good cause. Despite not being a law, it has the legal force and authority of law and cannot be arbitrarily revoked. It's up to the A.G. to decide whether it looks like something criminal occurred and might need to be investigated. Congress and the courts have no official role in appointing a federal prosecutor except they can use their power of influence elsewhere, especially in the media, to pressure the administration to hire a Special Prosecutor.

Department of Justice regulations are pretty relaxed on who that person should be. They state: "An individual named as Special Counsel shall be a lawyer with a reputation for integrity and impartial decision-making, and with appropriate experience to ensure both that the investigation will be conducted ably, expeditiously and thoroughly, and that investigative and prosecutorial decisions will be supported by an informed understanding of the criminal law and Department of Justice policies.

"The Special Counsel shall be selected from outside the United States Government. Special Counsels shall agree that their responsibilities as Special Counsel shall take first precedence in their professional lives, and that it may be necessary to devote their full time to the investigation, depending on its complexity and the stage of the investigation."

Special Prosecutors are taxpayer-funded travesties whose investigations carry on years after the public has lost interest, or the person they were appointed to investigate has left office. Their investigations almost never lead to the prosecution of the original target. This is because Special Counsels get to decide when, if ever, their investigations are over, and whether or not formal charges are being pursued. So if they don't get the guy they really want, they can save face—and still inflict some damage on the target—by fishing for petty, meaningless, irrelevant petty crimes committed by anyone who's ever had any contact with the target. Hence the Mueller prosecutions you've heard so much about, not one of which has a thing to do with Russia.

President Clinton's Whitewater scandal, which involved corruption between the Clintons and real estate developers while Bill was governor of Arkansas, is a perfect example of Special Counsel mission creep. A Special Prosecutor was appointed in 1992. He didn't formally conclude his investigation until 2003, also overshadowed by the other Special Prosecutor investigating the Lewinsky scandal. Neither Bill nor Hillary were ever prosecuted over Whitewater, naturally. But the investigation hung in the air for what felt like forever.

Nixon's Special Prosecutor stayed on board after Nixon resigned to investigate Gerald Ford, the new *de facto* President, for campaign finance violations, a job he wasn't hired to do. He ultimately found no wrongdoing, but that doesn't mean the active investigation had no effect on Ford's presidency. The Clinton years saw a third need for the appointment of a Special Prosecutor, this to investigate the handling of the A.T.F. and F.B.I. raid on the Waco, Texas compound housing Branch Davidian separatist cultists.

In 2003, the George W. Bush administration hired a Special Prosecutor to look into the Plame scandal, in which a journalist publicly outed the secret identity of C.I.A. agent Valerie Plame. Plame's husband had written an op-ed for the *New York Times* doubting President Bush's claim that Iraq was seeking uranium from Africa in the buildup to the invasion in 2003. No charges were filed for the leak itself, despite a criminal investigation, but former advisor to Vice President Dick Cheney, Scooter Libby, was convicted of lying to investigators. His prison sentence was commuted by Bush, and he was pardoned by Trump in 2018.

Robert Mueller was the next time in American politics a federal Special Prosecutor was appointed. Until Nixon, Special Prosecutors were almost always hired by the President to investigate and weed-out corruption in his own office, the executive branch. 238 people were indicted, with 110 being convicted, under Ulysses Grant's "Whiskey Ring" scandal. Roosevelt appointed Special Prosecutors to address two scandals, one involved allegations of bribery at the Post Office Department and another led to the indictments of nearly the entire state of Oregon's congressional delegation for a land grant scandal. When Harry Truman's Special Prosecutor investigating corruption at the Bureau of Internal Revenue was fired by his own Attorney General, Truman fired his

A.G., then appointed someone new in order to complete the investigation.

But these days, they're used for quite different purposes: As political cudgels with which to beat a President from the opposing party. Get a Special Counsel to chase down a few rumors and whether or not he gets the President impeached, you can count on a dozen of the President's colleagues, advisors and drinking buddies getting ten years because some vile bastard with an ax to grind in law enforcement asked them a gotcha question in a sworn interview. Sure, one or two of them will be bad dudes. I have no doubt Paul Manafort has been up to all kinds of heinous shit for decades. But the net will also catch people like Roger Stone.

* * *

Stone was asked six hundred questions in a matter of two or three hours when he volunteered to testify in front of a House committee. He did so of his own volition, without the need for a subpoena. And, boy, was he rewarded for that fateful act of generosity.

To secure the search warrants for Roger Stone's e-mail, text messages, and phone calls, as well as his home and office in Florida and his New York City apartment, prosecutors lied. It might shock you to hear me make the claim as boldly and bluntly as that. But it is true—and it is by no means the only time they did during their persecution of Stone. In the case of the warrants, prosecutors told a federal judge that they had probable cause for a variety of bizarre and unlikely crimes, such as money laundering of foreign funds into American campaign contributions, mail fraud, wire fraud and a smorgasbord of computer crimes, including unauthorized access to a server.

None of this was true. The sole evidence used to concoct this laundry list of imaginary offenses was Roger Stone's public Twitter feed, in which he taunted, mocked and provoked his political adversaries using innuendo, witty barbs and *aperçus*, facts he had gleaned from public news sources and, occasionally, good, old-fashioned name-calling. Stone later told reporters that the content on his Twitter feed was gleaned from entirely public sources. Needless to say, no evidence of any of these extraordinary and multifarious crimes was ever discovered and no charges were brought in respect of any of these fanciful allegations.

Instead, Stone was indicted for lying to Congress and for one count of witness tampering, which, as we shall see, is perhaps the most outrageous misrepresentation of innocent written communication in the history of American jurisprudence. This indictment, cobbled together after hundreds of hours of F.B.I. agents' time spent pouring over the six hundred answers Stone gave to Congress, was a pathetic end to the failed Mueller quest to prove collusion with Russia on the part of the Trump campaign.

Not a single one of the charges levelled at Stone had anything to do with Russia, WikiLeaks, foreign powers or money. It was a list of petty, victimless process crimes derived from an illegitimate and disastrous investigation whose central claims have been comprehensively disproven time and again.

Stone's indictment, which included a fantastical claim of witness tampering because Stone had discussed the Mueller investigation, and the F.B.I.'s subsequent persecution of Trump's former associates, with his on-off friend Randy Credico, was, after a dark fashion, a work of art. It was written by the architect and prime mover of the Mueller investigation, Andrew Weissman. Weissman had been the driving force behind many of the vindictive secondary prosecutions arising from the Special Counsel's slow-motion car crash, which failed to prove either collusion or obstruction of justice by the President.

Of course, this being the federal government, there were always going to be a few boneheaded slip-ups. When Roger Stone's indictment was emailed out to the press at 7 a.m. on the day of his arrest, a full two-and-a-half hours before a federal magistrate formally unsealed it, reporters and the Stone legal team noticed that the government had forgotten to wipe metadata that showed Weissman's initials, identifying him as the author of the document. Weissman, many Mueller targets have since told journalists privately, was the true guiding intelligence behind the report.

Robert Mueller, drafted in for his sterling reputation in Washington, D.C., was merely the face of the investigation, lending it his imprimatur and authority. As America became painfully aware during Mueller's cringeworthy, halting testimony to the House Intelligence Committee, it's not clear that the Special Counsel had even read the report that bore his name before it was published. Maybe he still hasn't.

CHAPTER TWO:
A HEART OF STONE

I'd met Roger Stone in person only once before, when he'd taken me to supper in New York City to a restaurant called the Beach Café on Manhattan's Upper East Side. These days, all of New York is enemy territory, and the Beach Café is one of the only places high-profile G.O.P. supporters and conservative personalities can go and not worry about being assaulted, shrieked at, or asked by the restaurant's own staff to leave.

Stone is on first-name terms with everyone, in the charming way a beloved regular is. He has a favorite table and usually orders the same meal directly from the owner, who almost literally fell over himself to wish Stone farewell. After dinner, we retired to Stone's *pied-à-terre*, where he gave me my first cigar on his roof terrace. I made a complete mess of trying to smoke it, about which Roger was very kind. I have not touched one since.

But when I later, after our friendship had deepened, accepted an invitation to dinner at his home in Fort Lauderdale in Florida, I wasn't sure what to expect. Over the years, I have collected a lot of eccentric, rich, famous and scandalous friends. It's a hobby, but also an inevitability for an eccentric. As a weirdo, I attract other weirdos. Fly-paper for freaks, as my grandmother used to say. But Roger Stone was an unknown quantity. I was fascinated by what sort of home life the notorious political operative and—as the media insists on calling him—dirty trickster had constructed for himself.

I was stunned by the normalcy of what I walked into. But not just the quotidian regularity of a loving home, a devoted and gorgeous wife, Nydia, and resplendent furnishings. I was mostly taken aback by the man I found in Stone's living room when we were quietly ushered inside. He was in a wheelchair, and his name was "Bob," and it was explained to me in matter-of-fact language that the Stone family had discovered Bob living in penury and filth on his own and taken him in, out of Christian charity.

When Roger and Nydia Stone met Bob in a church social group, he had no family left to provide for him. He was struggling to survive on his own. The Stones took responsibility for him, paying for his care at a succession of homes, none of which met Nydia's compassionate but exacting standards. Eventually, the Stones simply moved him into the house, welcoming him into the family. He became a permanent fixture in their living room—fed, watered, his medical needs satisfied.

Roger Stone is a battled-hardened veteran strategist for dozens of Republican politicians and a highly prolific and successful author and pundit in his own right and author of a *New York Times*-bestselling book about Lyndon B. Johnson. He has been a consultant for the Trump Organization for decades. He is also, as most people know, a former aide to Bob Dole, as well as Presidents Nixon and Reagan. He has a reputation for being ruthless, playing dirty and crushing his enemies.

I give you this potted history because the Bob thing isn't the sort of biographical detail you expect to read about one of Washington, D.C.'s most notoriously ruthless characters. It's certainly not the picture painted by the F.B.I. of a duplicitous charlatan. The authorities presented a few isolated text messages and emails, wrenched from context to make Stone seem like a habitually dishonest bully, threatening interlocutors and gleefully intimidating fragile acquaintances, to draw this sketch, knowing that a female jury would clutch their pearls at the sight of a bit of hyper-masculine bravado and balderdash. But this is simply at odds with the reality of the man Roger Stone.

Then again, he has always possessed a talent for presentation. Looking back at the etiology of Stone, his development into performance artist appears, as with so much of Stone's history, pre-ordained. Born to Gloria Stone and Roger J. Stone in late August of 1952 in Norwalk, Connecticut, Roger J. Stone, Jr. grew up in Lewisboro, New York. Raised in a working-class Catholic household, he was from adolescence taught to be both dutiful and family-oriented.

But that doesn't mean his home life was dull. Not many people know that Stone's parents were heavily involved in the local community theater—Stone, Sr. on a regular basis. Those who know Roger, as I do, have seen him assume many different guises over the years. But even earlier in his life, from grade-school mischief-maker to teenage operative for Richard Nixon, the early years for Stone, the ones in which he cut his political teeth, relied on theatrical skills he had picked up from his actor parents.

Stone is sometimes called as a "self-described" dirty trickster. I suppose he may have used the phrase dirty trickster about himself once or twice, but really "self-described" is a lie journalists add to a description of you they like, to give it some verisimilitude. They know no one will bother to check. As best I can tell, "dirty trickster" was first applied to Stone in 2008 by C.N.N. contributor Jeffrey Toobin in a story for the *New Yorker*.

Toobin is a pudgy and stupid person who was at that time a staff writer for the magazine. But I have to confess it's not entirely off the mark. Toobin was clearly over-whelmed by Stone's choice of meeting place—a sex club called Miami Velvet—and his hagiographic profile is worth reading in full for eyes-bulging-out-of-the-sockets moments like Toobin learning that Stone has had his suits tailor-made since the 1970s, something that left the drearily unkempt Toobin wide-eyed with awe.

Let me give you my own brief history of Stone's career, so you can understand the kind of guy we're talking about. Roger Stone's gift for subterfuge and trickery first emerged when he was just eight years old, so goes the legend, during the 1960 presidential elections. His elementary school held a mock-election for the students, where Stone helped sway the student vote for J.F.K.

As immortalized in one of Netflix's most-watched documentaries, *Get Me Roger Stone,* Stone learned the power of disinformation by spreading a rumor in the school cafeteria that Richard Nixon wanted to extend the school week to include Saturdays. Kennedy, who Stone said he liked more because he had better hair, won in a landslide, according to a local newspaper that covered the vote.

Four short years after the Nixon maneuver, Roger would experience his awakening to conservatism when a neighbor handed him a copy of Barry Goldwater's iconic Right-wing handbook, *The Conscience of a Conservative.* He devoured the book in a day and immediately resolved to attend the Republican National Convention. Stone points to Goldwater's book as the moment he realized he no longer wanted to be an actor, but instead wanted to be in politics. This infatuation with Goldwater would stay with him his entire life.

Stone is many things, but halfway-in or halfway-out is not one of them. He is also one of the most resilient and loyal people that I have ever known. Long after Goldwater's election defeat, a Goldwater sticker remained on his bicycle, and a campaign button in his lapel. "I was defiant," he has recalled over the years.

The remainder of high school was quieter for the provocateur. But then Stone got into George Washington University, a prestigious college deep in the D.C. swamp. This would prove to the formative period for Stone: He would meet his first wife and start sharpening his political toolkit while also insinuating himself onto Richard Nixon's infamous Committee to Re-Elect the President (C.R.E.E.P.).

Ann Wesche, Stone's first wife, explains in *Get Me Roger Stone* that the precocious, barely twenty-something student was already convincing grown men to run for office. His dorm room became the war room of a burgeoning political mover and shaker. His studies began to suffer as Stone fielded calls from clients, who would phone at all hours asking for advice on how to win their elections. These were the first stretches and yawns of a young man who would later become a kingmaker.

Stone's time at university came to an abrupt end in 1972, when Nixon adviser Herb Bart Porter visited the campus and asked him to join Nixon's re-election campaign. Released from his schooling and intoxicated by politics, Stone never looked back. And it was around this time that the mischief-maker was fully unleashed.

One of Roger's first tasks as an operative under Porter turned into one of his early masterpieces of sabotage. With direction from Porter and a dash of signature Stone *sprezzatura*, he delivered a contribution purporting to be from Nixon's primary opponent, Pete McKluskey of New Hampshire, to the Young Socialist Alliance. The receipt for the contribution was of course leaked to the *New Hampshire Daily Ledger* and other local newspapers ate it up.

And then there was Watergate. At just nineteen years old, Stone was named during the Watergate hearings as someone who had received money from a secret fund tied to Nixon's re-election efforts. Grinning from ear to ear in *Get Me Roger Stone*, Stone reminisced on how his parents were terrified, but that he was "having the time of his life."

That said, the years after Watergate were Stone's first wilderness years, during which he became a political wanderer in Washington with other Nixonites left jobless and untouchable by polite society. Pins were circulated during this time that read: "Hire A Nixon Vet."

Conservatives with long careers don't have the sort of institutional support liberals do, so they tend to go through periods of boom and bust. Famous for a bit, in obscurity for a bit, famous for a bit, and finally, if they're lucky, some degree of stability towards the end. So it was with Nixon and Stone, whose arcs of hubris and nemesis were bound to one other. Unpredictability requires resilience—hence the Nixon quote Stone loves to share over cocktails with reporters: "A man isn't finished when he's defeated. He's finished when he quits."

In 1977, Roger Stone took over the nation's most prominent and consequential youth auxiliary wing of the Republican Party, and got himself elected as Chairman of the Young Republican National Committee. Stone was not in the mold of the country-club establishment kid the Republican Party usually favored. He was a Goldwater guy, earthy and battle-hardened, like the real-estate mogul friend he would later successfully help to crowbar into the White House. It was during this time that Stone met Paul Manafort, a future business partner in what would become known as the forefather of modern lobbying firms.

Stone formed N.C.P.A.C., the National Conservative Political Action Committee, which was the first of its kind—a forerunner to today's P.A.C.s. He pioneered the use of independent expenditures to launch scorched-earth ad campaigns, usually negative attack ads, on leading Democrats of the era. Through his success with this type of campaigning, Stone continued to build his profile and reputation.

His political efforts were largely successful and he claimed his first scalp in the 1978 election, when N.C.P.A.C. helped Republican candidate Ron Jespen of Indiana defeat incumbent Democrat Dick Clark by four points, despite polling showing Clark ahead by nearly thirty points just a few weeks beforehand. N.C.P.A.C. fundraised like crazy off the back of this win. That's when Stone really began blossoming as a power-broker. From his position with the Young Republicans and the take-no-prisoners tactics employed by N.C.P.A.C., he gained the access and connections he needed to secure a role in the 1980 presidential elections.

It was around this time that Stone met Manhattan realty king Donald J. Trump. Stone was appointed the Northeastern Regional Coordinator for Ronald Reagan's presidential campaign, in an area of the country previously regarded a no-man's-land for Republicans.

Even back then, it was hard for G.O.P. candidates to win there. Stone met the future President Trump after being introduced to Trump's lawyer, infamous mob attorney and former lead counsel for Senator Joseph McCarthy's hearings on Communism in the 1950s, Roy Cohn.

Trump raised money for, and provided office space to, the Reagan campaign, so they had somewhere to put a phone bank and somewhere to meet. Stone would later tell friends that he had already sensed something special in Donald Trump, and resolved to maintain the friendship. Relatedly, it was during Reagan's 1980 campaign that Stone first identified the "Reagan Democrat," blue-collar Catholic voters leading similar lives to his parents. These voters would help Reagan win in a landslide against first-termer Jimmy Carter, a former peanut farmer whom many assumed would walk away with the majority of working-class votes.

Following Reagan's victory, Stone was tasked with conveying memos between former President Nixon and the newly installed Ronald Reagan. Stone thus became a central player in Washington, which enabled him to build his lobbying firm, Black, Manafort & Stone, into a money-printing operation. The *New Yorker*'s Jeffrey Toobin has said that Black, Manafort & Stone created "the modern, sleaze-ball lobbyist." That's about right. Stone and his partners were the first in the business to consult on a campaign, get the person elected, and then continue to provide access to the elected candidate. Stone's answer to people whining about conflicts of interest was: "Fuck it."

Black, Manafort & Stone also took on work for foreign dictators, including Mohamed Siad Barre of Somalia, Ferdinand Marcos of the Philippines, Mobutu Sese Seko of Zaire, and Jonas Savimbi of Angola. Stone began to show up at cocktail parties in silk slippers and bespoke suits, unashamed and unrepentant about his client list.

By the late 1980s, after briefly assisting Trump on the latter's casino ventures in New Jersey, Stone plucked up the courage to tell his friend that he should consider running for President. Trump made the trip to Portsmouth, New Hampshire, where it was speculated that he might announce a bid. Trump also teased the idea on an episode of Oprah Winfrey's talk show. This interview is regularly cited by Trump supporters to rebut accusations that the President has shifted political allegiance over the years. Ultimately, Trump's instincts told him it was not the right time.

In 1989, when Stone was headed to meet with Trump to discuss casino business, he convinced the Don to stay put and wait for him to travel from New York to New Jersey so they could form a game plan together on the way. Trump had been set to depart earlier, with several executives of his casino empire, on a helicopter. You might remember that helicopter as the one that went down, killing everyone on board. The chopper crashed into a wooded median of the Garden State Parkway. Stephen Hyde, who ran Trump's three Atlantic City casinos, Mark Etess, who managed the Trump Taj Mahal, and Johnathan Benanav, Executive Vice President of Trump Plaza, were killed, together with the two pilots.

Trump's lucky escape, and Roger Stone's hand in saving him, was divine providence, Stone later wrote. In his 2017 book *Making of the President: How Donald Trump Orchestrated A Revolution*, Stone says this was the moment that he realized Trump was predestined to become President and to "save" America. Stone also became convinced that he was ordained to help. To this day, Stone, who says he has narrowly escaped half a dozen plane and helicopter crashes, refuses to board a "puddle jumper," those small dual-prop passenger planes you sometimes take in the Bahamas.

In 1992, Roger Stone wed Nydia Bertran, a photographer he had known through her work for the Reagan campaign in the 1980s. He had met his match. Nydia was a fiery Cuban exile not afraid to speak her mind. In *Get Me Roger Stone*, Nydia explains how she employs her belief in Buddhism to "center" her husband, to which he quips back: "You mean censor." Trump was present at their wedding, as Stone has been at several of Trump's.

A brief sex scandal in the 1990s put Stone out of circulation for a while. He was caught placing classified ads for a third sex partner to join him and his wife. It was the era of the "values voter," and the sexually libertine Stone found himself completely out of step with the social mores of the Republican Party for the first time in two decades.

Stone stepped down from his role on the Bob Dole campaign and sat it out until 2000, when he returned to the idea of Trump running for President with new energy. Trump, toying with a run for the Reform Party, slammed his then-opponent Pat Buchanan as a "Hitler lover" and someone who "hates the blacks, doesn't like the Jews or the gays." He torched Buchanan's chances, and then left the race, a scheme some say was cooked up by Stone to make sure Dubya had no serious challengers. The party had learned its lesson from Ross Perot.

Despite writing a book called *The Bush Crime Family*, Stone was instrumental in having a Miami-Dade recount stopped in 2000 with the so-called "Brooks Brothers riot," a brief skirmish he helped to organize featuring well-groomed local Republicans that shut down the recount station. The recount never started back up again at that particular polling station, one of the two or three factors that cost Gore the election.

For many East Coast Democrats today, Stone is a figure of hatred thanks to one particular job: Taking down Spitzer. New York Governor Elliot Spitzer had a thing about prostitutes, and, in 2008, Stone was responsible for bringing the Governor down by leaking incriminating and mesmerizing details to the press, including the fact that Spitzer liked to keep his socks on during intercourse, and that he sometimes choked girls beyond their comfort level. And, of course, by referring Spitzer to the police.

That heady, indulgent 2008 *New Yorker* profile I mentioned earlier describes Stone like this: "For nearly forty years, Stone has hovered around Republican and national politics, both near the center and at the periphery. At times, mostly during the Reagan years, he was a political consultant and lobbyist who, in conventional terms, was highly successful, working for such politicians as Bob Dole and Tom Kean. Even then, though, Stone regularly crossed the line between respectability and ignominy, and he has become better known for leading a colorful personal life than for landing big-time clients."

Today, the Stones have two grown children and five grandchildren. They are parishioners at Saint Anthony's Catholic Church in Fort Lauderdale. Bob died a year or so after I first met him at dinner in Fort Lauderdale. He is buried in Florida. The Stone family paid for all his funeral expenses.

CHAPTER THREE: MEET AMY

When you step into Courtroom 3 on the second floor of the Washington, D.C. District Court, you are confronted with a huge slab of gray marble covering most of the far wall. Set into the marble is a large seal. It reads: United States District Court, District of Columbia. To the left of the marble wall is a flag; to the right, a door, from which the judge and the jury emerge. A clock with two bare steel hands silently counts time. To any patriot, this monument to American jurisprudence ought to be moving, or in some way humbling, but it is not, because those who are here for Roger Stone's trial know that everything in this place is rotten.

The air is damp and hot. Dog-eared copies of *U.S.A. Today* tumble off the pews. *U.S.A. Today* is a newspaper for people who are not allowed to express their political opinions at work but who wish they could; it is ghastly and everything about it, and in it, is a lie. The people who read it, the sort of people who work for the federal government, are bitter and hopeless, and you can tell from their taste in interior design. Around the court-room runs wood paneling of the kind you often see in federal buildings. It is covered in nicks and marks and scratches, in a state of neglect. The wood is recycled mahogany from another courthouse, and it makes the room feel like an assembly hall at a public school. This is not a happy place. No one should have to be here.

Judge Amy Berman Jackson, presiding over this case, has a blue and white porcelain lamp on her bench. It is never switched on, but she glances at it all the time, which must mean it came to her from someone who is now dead. Someone with bad taste; the lamp is horrible. I'm watching her give instruction to the government lawyers. With the white noise machine switched on, she is opaque—impossible to read. Even when you can hear her, Jackson has the personality of stodgy fruit pudding and the countenance to match. She has a man's face, but a man's face left out in the sun, as though she has one of those floppy silicon serial killer masks permanently stitched to her head.

Despite this, she is unremarkable, and her hair makes me gag. She comes across like a woman with no gay friends, which for a Democrat in the twenty-first century is unthinkable. If it weren't for the three loud knocks on the door and an "All rise!" I don't think anyone would notice Amy Berman Jackson walk into a room. Maybe that's why she became a judge, so people can't pretend they don't see her.

I'm given to wondering why Jackson chose to become a federal judge, because after watching this case unfold I doubt she is much motivated by the pursuit of justice. The government went to great lengths to lock in the right judge for this case, and the Obama-appointed Jackson did not disappoint them. Where she has not outright sabotaged the defense with repressive and outlandish restrictions on what kinds of arguments they can make, she has shredded the First Amendment to muzzle Stone and his friends from speaking about the trial, robbing him of the ability to defend himself against the damage done by this politically motivated prosecution and denying him the right to clear his name.

Special Counsel prosecutors wanted Amy Berman Jackson for the Stone trial, so they claimed that Stone's case was related to a still-untried case in which Mueller charged seventy-five Russians for the alleged hacking of the Democratic National Committee. The pretext was that Stone's emails had shown up thanks to a search warrant in that case. Mueller's office argued that the cases were related because "stolen documents" were a factor in both trials, and because the warrants in the Russian case surfaced "certain evidence that is relevant" to Stone's case. Needless to say, no such evidence was ever produced, at trial or elsewhere. It was all a lie.

Nothing in Stone's indictment suggested that he had access to stolen documents, but via this legal maneuver, Mueller and his team was allowed to "judge shop" for the member of the bench most likely to throw the book at Stone. Amy Berman Jackson had previously presided over Paul Manafort's trial, during which Manafort was denied bail before and after the case was heard, even though he hadn't been convicted of any crime and even placed in solitary, for no apparent reason. A motion for a different judge and a different venue by Stone's lawyers was of course denied.

Ahead of the trial, Jackson banned Stone from pointing out that he was being selectively prosecuted and singled out for special treatment, despite copious evidence that former Director of National Intelligence James Clapper, former F.B.I. Director James Comey, former F.B.I. agent Peter Strzok and former deputy F.B.I. Director Andrew McCabe all lied to Congress, and despite the Mueller report affirming that multiple witnesses lied to the Special Counsel. None of these people has been held to account for their flagrant and repeated untruths, even though their errors and omissions were far more substantial and egregious—not to mention on purpose.

In every single motion bar one, Jackson ruled against Stone's lawyers in favor of the federal government. And she went to extraordinary lengths to cripple his defense, kneecapping his defense team by proscribing every promising avenue of argument for a variety of batty reasons. Jackson even barred Stone's lawyers from asking whether the Democratic National Committee was, in fact, hacked by the Russians. Stone says the evidence is scant, and that the government is relying on a report from a Clinton-adjacent cybersecurity firm called Crowd-Strike.

The F.B.I. admits it never bothered to inspect the D.N.C.'s servers itself, which is highly unusual. It seems they just took CrowdStrike's word for it, accepting as fact a one-page summary the firm provided and some vague assertions printed in the *Washington Post*. When this irregularity was pointed out during discovery, the government hastily filed a motion claiming that it had independent verification of the hack originating in Russia, but refused to give the specifics or to provide any evidence.

There is widespread speculation that it wasn't even a hack at all that produced those emails, but rather a leak from inside the D.N.C. by disgruntled Bernie Sanders supporter Seth Rich, who was shortly afterwards murdered in cold blood outside his Washington, D.C. home. Rich's murder remains unsolved.

The government wanted any discussion of the hack— or leak, if you prefer—excluded from trial because Stone's arguments partly rest on his doubt that Russia was responsible for the D.N.C. hack. If he sincerely believed Russia wasn't responsible at the time he gave his answers to Congress, then he cannot be guilty of lying about having more Russia-related emails, because Wikileaks, in his mind, had nothing to do with Russia. He would have complied with the Committee's demands to answer "within the publicly announced parameters" of their investigation, a condition he negotiated ahead of time. Judge Jackson happily complied with the government's request, fatally weakening a central plank of Stone's defense strategy.

The chief prosecutor in Stone's case was Jeannie Rhee, a lawyer and a Democrat fixture who represented Hillary Clinton during the private email server scandal and on another occasion represented the Clinton Foundation, and who gave the maximum allowable donation to Hillary Clinton in both 2008 and 2016, as well as donating to Barack Obama. Naturally, Stone was barred from raising this as a conflict of interest during the trial, despite the obvious loathing everyone involved in bringing this case has for him and for the President, which explains the vindictive and wasteful crusade against Trump's associates since it became clear the Mueller Report was a bust.

In this and a thousand other ways, the defense was crippled from day one by Amy Berman Jackson, whose greatest hits include dismissing the wrongful death suit filed against Hillary Clinton by two Benghazi parents in 2017 and, four years before that, playing fast and loose with the religious liberty of the Catholic Church over contraception provisions in Obamacare.

Jackson describes herself as nonpartisan, but in February 2020 she leapt to criticize President Trump and Fox News host Tucker Carlson for expressing perfectly ordinary and widely-held opinions about the case. "The President of the United States used his Twitter platform to disseminate a point of view about a juror," she noted disapprovingly at Stone's sentencing. " 'Now it looks like the foreperson in the jury in the Roger Stone case has significant bias.' And that was printed in the *Washington Post* on February 13, 2020. He also repeated at a televised rally, according to newsweek.com, that the foreperson was jumping up and down at the guilty verdict."

As will become clear in the following chapter, there can be no doubt that the jury foreperson, a lifelong Democrat activist and one-time Congressional candidate, was celebrating her "win" getting Stone convicted. But Jackson scolded the President for singling her out. "In a highly polarized political climate in which the President himself has shone a spotlight on the jury through his use of social media, which doesn't just reach those who follow him on Twitter but also gets reported in the news media, the risk of harassment and intimidation of any jurors who may testify in the hearing scheduled for later today or in juror misconduct is extremely high and that individuals who may be angry about Mr. Stone's conviction or other developments in the news may choose to take it out on them personally."

It's true that Trump's social media incontinence can sometimes harm as much as it helps. But, last I checked, it was crazed Left-wing gunmen who shot Steve Scalise in 2017, shot up the Family Research Council after reading about it on the S.P.L.C. in 2012, shot up an I.C.E. detention center (*passim*), shot and killed nine people in Dayton, O.H. in August 2019, and shot up YouTube's headquarters in 2018. We're still waiting patiently for the appearance of those much-fêted Trump-enabled Right-wing death squads. It doesn't matter how many times liberals show up with guns determined to kill someone— or how many people they actually do kill—all the press ever wants to talk about is Charlottesville and Heather Heyer, and how dangerous Republicans are.

Jackson repeatedly took aim at Tucker Carlson throughout February 2020, because he had, "Accused the foreperson of the jury of being an anti-Trump zealot and broadcast on the screen her Twitter handle and other personal information. Mr. Carlson added, 'This is not a neutral person. This is not someone capable of judging this trial fairly. This is a partisan who lied about who she was.' He concluded, Roger Stone is facing life in prison because an Obama-appointed judge, Amy Berman Jackson, allowed this woman to run the jury." So far, so accurate, Judge Jackson.

To really understand just what a great fit Judge Jackson was for the Stone trial, you have to go back a bit. Born in Baltimore and a graduate of Harvard Law, Jackson is a pedigreed member of the elites. Her father was a well-known physician working at Johns Hopkins, and Jackson was set up for life from birth, born into the kind of liberal privilege for which ordinary conservative voters have so much contempt.

After graduation and doing a few clerkships, Jackson landed her first major job as an Assistant United States Attorney in the District of Columbia, a role she held from 1980 to 1986. She worked in precisely the office that would, thirty-five years later, bring Stone's case. But Jackson also had private-sector law firm experience, and that's where things get interesting. Because Jackson and Roger Stone have history, kind of.

Jackson worked at Venable, Baetjer & Howard, L.L.P., a prestigious law firm that counts former U.S. senator Birch Bayh among its most well-known partners. Bayh was famously defeated by Dan Quayle for a fourth term in the United States Senate, in large part thanks to the Roger Stone-backed N.C.P.A.C. Amy Berman Jackson's favorite boss, for whom she worked for years, got his ass handed to him by a barely thirty-year-old Roger Stone.

Maybe it's a stretch to assume any lingering resentment. But when so many deep and close connections are *not* disclosed by the heavily incestuous denizens of the D.C. swamp, is it any wonder Stone allies have been asking questions?

Amy Berman Jackson would spend the rest of the late 1980s until 2010 in private practice, representing the likes of William J. Jefferson, the New Orleans-based Democrat congressman who is currently serving a long prison sentence for his role in accepting $400,000, for directing contracts to an ally, a crime that would catch up to him years after the F.B.I. raided his congressional offices in the late 2000s. It's too easy to chide defense attorneys for the sort of clients they represent, since everyone, guilty or otherwise, deserves good legal representation and a fair trial. But it's worth at least noting that Jackson represented one of the most corrupt Democrat politicians of the modern era. It's not like she was assigned the case as a public defender.

In 2010, President Obama nominated Jackson to fill a vacant seat on the United States District Court for the

District of Columbia, a nomination that would lapse at the end of 2010, although Obama would re-nominate her again in 2011 with success. President Obama was determined that Jackson should be appointed. Now we know why.

During her time as a D.C. federal judge, Jackson has handled her fellow Democrats with kid gloves. She gave Jesse Jackson, Jr. and his family lightweight sentences for stealing campaign money for personal expenses. The Jesse Jackson clan admitted to their crimes in plea deals and under oath. They nicked three quarters of a million dollars. What kind of time did Jackson settle on for this criminal duo? Less than three years.

Jackson used a somewhat rougher pair of gloves in her assessment of a case brought by the Catholic Church, which in 2013 wanted an exemption from Obamacare because of its requirement to provide birth control coverage, a clear violation of religious freedom. Jackson would repeatedly rule against the Church, foreshadowing her habitual bias in the Stone case, and delivering a *coup de grâce* in late 2013 by throwing out the entire lawsuit.

Before her role in that case, or Stone's, the most notable political decision Jackson made was her dismissal of a wrongful death suit against Hillary Clinton, brought by parents of dead service members from the Benghazi attack. That's the attack about which then-Secretary of State and future presidential candidate Clinton would proclaim, during a Congressional hearing, "What does it matter?" when asked why she did not send urgently-needed support to the besieged consulate during a 2012 Islamic militant attack on two U.S. government facilities in Libya. Jackson tossed the case.

2017 was the year of Jackson's infamous Benghazi decision, but it was also the year she hit the lottery with the fallout cases from fellow Clinton supporter Robert Mueller's failed investigation. By some extraordinary stroke of luck, Jackson got *four* of the Mueller prosecutions. Is she the luckiest woman on Earth? Of course not. We already know she was locked in by lying prosecutors who pretended cases were related that weren't, and who alluded to massive lists of federal crimes they had no intention of including on indictments, in order to get their preferred jurist.

Federal judges and prosecutors, though you might perceive them to be under public records laws like other elected or appointed officials in the government, operate in total secrecy. We can never know how many briefings, phone calls or strategy directives Amy Berman Jackson got from prosecutors, investigators, or helpful members of the intelligence community. But we can guess, and the number isn't zero.

As the world knows, Jackson threw the book at Paul Manafort, the former Trump campaign Chairman and one-time business associate of Roger Stone, sending him on a one-way trip to solitary confinement even before he'd been convicted of anything, despite the fact that he had no history of violence and didn't appear to be a flight risk. To be fair, Manafort does seem like a piece of shit and he probably did it all and deserves to spend some time behind bars. But more intriguing is that Jackson also took care of Rick Gates's trial—the same Gates who would sing like a canary, as they say, at the Stone trial, telling the jury whatever he thought the government wanted to hear in order to get a shorter sentence for himself.

The election of Donald Trump really fucked things up for Washington, D.C. They've never gotten over it and they never will. But the city might at least have made a decent show of putting on a fair trial for Jackson's next job, which was Stone. Even though the judge had ruled in favor of Hillary Clinton, whose candidacy was badly damaged by Stone's book *The Clintons' War on Women*, and even though the judge was a two-time donor to Clinton, federal judges are federal judges and, for the most part, operate as a law unto themselves—which became obvious when Jackson was allowed to decide for herself whether she should be recused from the case.

Is it me, or is something a bit off there? Political revenge is supposed to occur, in America at least, at the ballot box. Not through Soviet-style show trials.

The way you know Jackson was a catastrophe for any Republican defendant was that the press rushed to print quivering encomiums about her as soon as the first Republican dared to utter her name. On February 20, 2020, the day of Stone's sentencing, N.B.C. Los Angeles produced a glowing tribute to Jackson, quoting a female Harvard law professor who described the judge as "made of steel."

N.B.C. also quoted a criminal defense lawyer who calls her "whip-smart... a first-rate federal judge." The lawyer in question has a son who is also a federal judge, Jon Tigar. The younger Tigar had, just coincidentally, been harshly criticized by Trump for his rulings on asylum seekers a few months previously.

But don't just take your opinion of Amy Berman Jackson from her fellow lawyers. Take it from Judge Jackson's own family. Her son, Matt Jackson, is a paralegal who won thirteen consecutive games of *Jeopardy!* in 2015, taking home $413,612, the fifth-highest total ever won on the program in regular, non-tournament play. Matt Jackson became a brief internet sensation thanks to an unnervingly slow smile that crept across his ogrish, stubby face. Unprompted, he described his mother on the show as "white, liberal and Jewish."

Judge Jackson insisted during sentencing that Roger Stone, "Has not been prosecuted by his adversary or anyone else's adversary, and he was not prosecuted to enable anyone to gain political advantage. This case did not arise because Roger Stone was being pursued by his political enemies. It arose because Roger Stone, characteristically, injected himself smack into the center of one of the most significant issues of the day." The horror!—The *chutzpah!* You can smell the snobbery from across state lines.

But while she maintained, with a straight face, that the grounds for bringing charges against Stone were above board and nonpartisan, Jackson could not help heaping scorn on his character, career history and judgment. "The defense, in its allocution, talked about not paying too much attention to his persona, but the defendant chose it and cultivated it. And I was told that the publicity and attention swirling around this case has already caused considerable stress for the defense and his family, but he was at the heart of a great deal of it. Through his press conferences and social media posts, he made the choice to stoke it."

"Certain themes emerged, even from the people who submitted letters on his behalf attached to his memo," she added. "There are letters that tell me he cultivated a career image of a bare-knuckled brawler in politics. One friend and letter writer wrote: He's a provocateur who enjoyed, even relished, the spotlight. They called him a dirty trickster, a political hit man."

"These are the people who wrote on his behalf," Jackson quipped, and although she didn't quite add, *So this has been a long time coming and you can't say he didn't ask for it*, her estimation was hanging in the air, just the same, for all to see and hear.

In case listeners were in any doubt, Jackson tacked on a coded reference to Hell to signal her true feelings about Stone's moral character, and perhaps even to tweak him for being Christian. "It's important to note today, though, to the people who emphasized this side of the defendant, that I am not passing judgment on Roger Stone as a man. That falls to a higher authority." Even the most obtuse listener in the gallery had got the message by then.

No liberal in good standing can let a week pass without a stab at fainting-couch victimhood, and Judge Jackson is no exception, though it was never clear whether her protestations about the dangers of public opinion were sincerely felt, or just an excuse to punish Stone. When a social media intern posted a photograph and caption critical of Jackson to Stone's Instagram account—which unfortunately happened to feature a step-and-repeat board logo vaguely reminiscent of crosshairs in the vicinity of, though not on top of, an image of the judge—Jackson leapt at the opportunity to muzzle Stone from making any further criticism of her political biases or her history of Left-wing judgments.

"By deliberately stoking public opinion against prosecution and the Court in this matter, he willfully increased the risk that someone else, with even poorer judgment than he has, would act on his behalf," Jackson thundered. "This is intolerable to the administration of justice, and the Court cannot sit idly by, shrug its shoulder and say: Oh, that's just Roger being Roger, or it wouldn't have grounds to act the next time someone tries it."

Jackson accused, and apparently continues to believe, that Stone had a book "wending its way to publishers" that he withheld from her, and which might have violated the terms of her gag order. This is not so. She was also prepared to believe just about any rumor her coterie of angry-looking (and here I confess I speculate) lesbian law clerks brought to her attention, such as a claim made by Alex Jones on his *InfoWars* radio program that Stone had reached out to him during the trial. This would have been a serious breach of the restrictions placed on him by Jackson.

Those of us who have been pals with Alex Jones for a few years know that friendship with him is a wondrous, magical and delicate thing. He is a kind, generous, hilarious, insightful and ferociously intelligent man. But there is always, and you have to factor this in to any interaction with him, the risk that he'll go "off script." I'm sure he won't mind me saying that. It's just something that happens when the passions are aroused, and few radio hosts in America are as emotionally engaged with their subject as Jones.

To be clear: Stone did not ever contact Jones during the trial. But it was enough for Jackson that Jones claimed it on his show, and it gave both the judge and prosecutors, who must have been keenly aware of the polarizing brand of *InfoWars*, an excuse to raise it once again in front of the jury. And, indeed, more than one juror audibly scoffed at the mere mention of it.

Alex Jones and his *InfoWars* network hold a special place in the liberal hate canon precisely because Jones says things no other host dares to, but which plenty of us wish we could and which in many cases we know to be true but cannot prove to the satisfaction of professional journalistic strictures.

The other thing you have to understand about *InfoWars* is that it's not a radio network in the convention sense. It is a ministry. In the same way that fire and brimstone preachers in Pentecostal churches hold forth about the homo-demons, sometimes literally, but more often using demons as a proxy for sin, Alex Jones uses language that is heavily metaphoric.

When he casually refers to lesbianism as Satanic, he's using "lesbian" as a stand-in for a variety of ugly progressive lifestyle choices, while at the same time correctly noting the over-representation of that class of person in, for instance, Gender Studies departments, which perpetuate the ungodly horrors of cultural Marxism.

Likewise, he uses "Satanic" in both its conventional sense and also to signal general moral condemnation. There's a lot going on and you have to be familiar with Jones's style to understand what he's getting at. But, when you understand all this, the Alex Jones phenomenon starts to make more sense.

Once you've listened to him for a while and you wrap your head around some the idiomatic delivery, he becomes compelling—and more easily understood. Jones's content relies on apocalyptic warnings, while the products he sells, such as the infamous Brain Force pills, are about salvation and healing, promising natural, scientifically-tested relief as an antidote to the poison on C.N.N. and in daily modern life.

Most of my friends will wince when I say this, but I find that when you cut through the preacher's rhetoric and understand that his true message is usually the underlying morality and not the surface detail—a bit like Trump, you might say—Alex Jones is maddeningly, incomprehensibly and inexplicably correct about almost everything he talks about, even if it's not obvious at the time, even if some of the specifics aren't quite right, and even if it takes years for him to be vindicated. With the possible exception, I guess, of Sandy Hook. You can have that one.

It's not a coincidence that the last half-decade of American public life has revolved around jesters, jokers and Fools such as Roger Stone, Alex Jones, Donald Trump and me, for the simple reason that in an age of stultifying conformity, we aren't boring. And it's not a coincidence that the same four people are the most hated men in America by a po-faced establishment that relies on meek compliance and the willing submission of the general public to enforce its orthodoxies.

It's not a coincidence that in an era of spiritual desolation, in which transcendence has been scrubbed from culture in favor of satisfying base appetites, and uplifting moral vision has been replaced by bogus earnestness in politics, that the most popular and dangerous figures in culture are all some combination of heroic archetype, true believer, teacher and prophet, and that all four have highly developed senses of humor trained on the ruling classes.

After all, tyrants—and judges—only maintain their illusion of authority by preventing people from laughing at them. The best tell I know, if you want to figure out whether someone's from the swamp? They can't stand being teased. All four of the men I mention have teased the establishment relentlessly, and been punished for it—but, in our chastisement, revealed that the hatred of the elites shows they have no real authority, only the power of fear and shame, which may feel real in this life, but which is ultimately empty, and the reason they all seem so... *gray*.

Finally, it's not a coincidence that Jones, Stone and your present correspondent all have Christ in common— nor that President Trump, whether he really believes or not, and who can say, has had the good sense to genuflect before God, the good instincts to recognize Christianity as the true basis of Western civilization, and the good judgment to ferociously defend Christian morality since the day he took office.

CHAPTER FOUR:
A JURY OF HIS PEERS

"I sat in the courtroom during Roger Stone's jury selection," wrote O.A.N.N. correspondent Jack Posobiec on Twitter on February 12, 2020. "Time and again his lawyers pointed out anti-Trump bias on the part of jurors, and one by one the judge dismissed their concerns." I was there too. Here's how it went down.

The first member of the jury pool to take the stand was a former Obama White House staffer who held a senior communications job, whose husband was a lawyer, working on national security policy for the Department of Justice, and who numbered among her close friends other lawyers working in the U.S. Attorney's office—the same office that was prosecuting this case.

Ordinarily, the mere fact of being a lawyer, or of being married to one, can be grounds for dismissal from a jury. Everyone knows what the effect of having a lawyer on a jury can be, especially if they end up as the foreman. Even if they don't identify themselves as such, lawyers will immediately command the room with their superior knowledge of legal procedures and terminology. If another juror is overwhelmed by the details of the case, or cannot wrap their head around a technicality, they will tend to go along with the guy who sounds like he knows what he's talking about. Wouldn't you?

Plus, of course, lawyers are trained in the arts of persuasion and deception. Sometimes they don't even realize they're doing it. It's what they do for a living, after all. So if a lawyer enters a jury with precon- ceived opinions or biases that the judge doesn't catch, or chooses to overlook, or which the defense team fails to spot during its research, it can destroy any hope of a fair trial. As we will see, the Stone jury didn't just have a biased lawyer as its foreman. Half a dozen members of the jury were hopelessly conflicted and should never have been allowed to serve.

Custom and precedent get thrown out of the window, it seems, when the person on trial is Roger Stone. Judge Jackson declined to strike this first potential juror from the jury pool, insisting that her claim not to have any preconceived opinions about Stone was credible, and adding that she believed the juror could put her political opinions aside to render a fair verdict. Just reflect on that for a moment.

When Judge Jackson refused to send her home, there were audible gasps in the courtroom gallery. On most days, I sat in the family pew with Nydia Stone when attending trial. But, on this particular day, I'd sat in the back row—so I got to see the entire gallery of people gasp, then freeze in horror. Eventually, confused laughter rippled through the room as everyone looked at their neighbors in bewilderment.

Stone mentee and journalist Jacob Engels gave an interview to *InfoWars* to sound the alarm about this potential juror and the state of the jury selection process as a whole. Sharing this publicly available information almost landed him in jail. A sealed order of contempt was issued for Engels, who wisely did not enter the courtroom the next day. Jones and Engels had made a small error in their telling of the story: They said the Obama communications chief had been confirmed onto the jury, rather than merely admitted into the pool. They also, separately, misidentified another potential juror.

But they didn't do anything the wildly speculating pontificators on cable news weren't doing twenty-four hours a day. And besides, the central objection stood: If Jackson wouldn't strike this juror from the pool, who *would* she strike? Even the left-wing journalists in the room had to admit—and, privately, did—that it was an outrage.

In issuing the contempt order, Jackson, in concert with the prosecution, in effect wanted to arrest a journalist for discussing publicly available information about a potential juror. Hundreds of reporters had been discussing the backgrounds and even the possible identities of potential jurors during this process. Engels and

Jones went in hard with accusations of a rigged jury—allegations that turned out to be true! But they got a contempt order for their troubles.

The jury questionnaires and the names of those who served on the Stone jury remain under seal. This author has examined the unredacted questionnaires in detail since they were leaked to the public, presumably by an appalled member of the court staff, and I have been stunned by them. The public deserves to see these questionnaires and know the names of these jurors. The documents should be unsealed.

* * *

It gradually dawned on us that the entire pool was going to be a disaster. Even for the District of Columbia, the demographics were hopelessly hostile. As far as I could tell, there were no Irish, no Catholics, no veterans, no Republicans and no black men. The pool, as one of Stone's friends quipped, went "from lattes to chardonnays": white spinsters, angry-looking Hispanic women, skinny white soy-drinking beta males and a couple of black women who were making no secret of their irritation at being fingered for jury duty.

The pool demographics didn't match the rest of the country, but they also didn't match Washington, D.C. either. Talk about a jury of your peers. By some miraculous and improbable chain of coincidences and probabilities, the supposedly random and computerized jury selection process yielded a jury of single, middle-aged *Washington Post*-reading female lawyers in pantsuits. Just fancy that.

Criminal trial rules stipulate that guilty verdicts must be unanimous. Every member of the jury has to be sure beyond a reasonable doubt that the defendant is guilty, or he walks free. You might imagine that this rule would make convictions difficult to achieve. But the opposite is true: According to the Department of Justice, federal courts have a ninety-three per cent conviction rate as of 2012, up from eighty-five per cent a few decades earlier. In other words, if you're accused of a crime and the case makes it to trial, you're most likely to be found guilty, irrespective of the merits, and federal court is especially bad.

On the rare occasion defendants walk free, it's normally not because they had great lawyers, or made the best argument. Or because they're innocent. It's because one of the jurors refused to convict them for some other reason, or because the police screwed something up. That's why jury demographics are everything, and why the government went to so much trouble to stack the deck.

Before I learned about the political attitudes and biases of the Stone jury, I knew that prosecutors sometimes made politically-motivated decisions about whom to charge, and with what. I knew that judges had biases. I knew that the intelligence agencies were compromised, and politicized, and had been leveraged against Donald

Trump, probably illegally, to prevent him from winning the presidency in 2016, and that they were still up to no good.

But what I never imagined was that something as supposedly sacrosanct as randomized jury selection could be compromised in America, supposedly a land of laws and rules, where corruption was rooted out and punished. What I found out about the jury in the course of writing this book scandalized me, and it has irrevocably shaken my faith in the fairness of the American jurisprudential system.

* * *

In what follows, I have gone to great lengths to protect the identities of the jurors in question while not compromising essential details, even though I suspect some of them may not deserve the courtesy. Regardless of the fact that jury questionnaires have been posted on the internet by roguish Right-wing activists and are readily searchable, I am electing not to name any of the jurors, per Judge Jackson's entreaties and to avoid even the appearance of targeting them for any kind of retribution.

There are three exceptions to this rule. Juror Tomeka Hart and juror Seth Cousins both chose to reveal their identities to the world in editorials in the pages of the *Washington Post* and on Facebook, forfeiting their rights to privacy. Both have either given extensive media interviews or have been briefing journalists behind the scenes, especially Cousins, who appeared on C.N.N. to defend Hart against charges of bias from the President after she outed herself, and after her virulently anti-Trump and anti-Stone Twitter history came to light. It is also worth noting that Cousins admitted to the *Washington Post* that he was not really paying attention to arguments made by the defense.

Finally, juror Maureen O'Leary has been the subject of a *New York Times* story in which she sharply, and using foul language, criticized President Trump and the White House during a media-confected brouhaha about Hurricane Dorian. "'You are not going to believe this BULL,' Maureen O'Leary, a longtime public affairs specialist at N.O.A.A., wrote to a colleague. She followed up, relaying some of the most choice public comments she was finding including, 'Should I call the White House for my weather forecasts from now on?', adding an expletive." It would be negligent to exclude this public domain information.

Tomeka Hart and Seth Cousins—a bald, black spinster and an elderly gay man, respectively—have both insisted, at times ferociously, that the deliberations of the jury were the product of close and dispassionate examination of the evidence. "I believe I speak for my fellow jurors when I say we are proud of our decision. We listened carefully to the testimony of a series of witnesses and carefully examined every element of every charge and its defense, and we unanimously agreed that each had been proved beyond a reasonable doubt," Cousins wrote in the *Washington Post*.

But information I have since received casts doubt on the ability of the Stone jury to render an impartial verdict—and doubt, too, on several jurors' honesty in describing their feelings about the defendant and their own political biases.

To start with, the demographics of the jury read like a Hillary Clinton donor spreadsheet. Two jurors were homosexual men; one, Seth Cousins, publicly "out" of his own volition. The other homosexual man I will of course not name. Of the overwhelming number of women on the jury, four of them were thirty-eight years old or more, single and never married. And seven jurors had post-graduate degrees. That's fifty-eight per cent of the jury, compared with thirteen per cent of the general American population. No one under the age of thirty-eight served on the jury.

Out of twelve jurors, ten told the court they only watched Left-wing news sources, including the *New York Times*, the *Washington Post*, C.N.N., N.B.C. News, C.B.S. News, A.B.C. News, M.S.N.B.C, N.P.R., P.B.S. and even *HuffPost* and *Buzzfeed*. Not one juror mentioned any Right-leaning news source at all, even the phenomenally popular Fox News. Note that jurors were not asked which news sources they always agreed with; merely which, if any, they were accustomed to getting their news from. The only two jurors who did not cite Left-wing news sources said they watched local affiliate FOX 5 D.C.

Only three jurors admitted to following specific po-litical commentators. Among those listed were David

Brooks and Mark Shields on P.B.S. *Newshour*. One juror listed Anderson Cooper, Rachel Maddow and Chris Hayes as their most-watched T.V. news personalities. Another gave Anderson Cooper, Rachel Maddow and Lawrence O'Donnell. No conservative news hosts or commentators were listed by any jurors.

Despite all this self-described news junkery, jurors were remarkably circumspect about their pre-existing political opinions. Just two jurors admitted to having any opinions at all about any of the thirty-one names of prominent people involved in, or potentially referred to, in the case. Imagine, as you read this, saying you have no opinions *at all* about *any* of the following people.

1. Julian Assange
2. Jason Aubin
3. Steve Bannon
4. William Binney
5. Zachary Blevins
6. Matthew Boyle
7. Michael Caputo
8. Peter Clay
9. Hillary Clinton
10. Jerome Corsi
11. Randy Credico
12. Rick Gates
13. Jason Fishbein

14. David Gray

15. John Kakanis

16. Margaret Kunstler

17. David Lugo

18. Theodore Malloch

19. Paul Manafort

20. Rebekah Mercer

21. Andrew Miller

22. Tyler Nixon

23. Sam Nunberg

24. John Podesta

25. Alexandra Preate

26. Erik Prince

27. Bill Samuels

28. Michael Strum

29. Jason Sullivan

30. Michelle Taylor

31. Donald Trump

Unless you've been glued to cable news for the past five years, you perhaps recognized, say, five or ten names on that list. But let's just take those five or ten. We're being asked to believe that ten people out of twelve on a Washington, D.C. jury of news junkie Democrats have *no opinion at all* about Hillary Clinton, Donald Trump, Steve Bannon, former Blackwater C.E.O. Erik Prince and WikiLeaks founder Julian Assange.

I can find you high school track stars in Ohio who don't own televisions who nonetheless have choice things to say about these five very famous people.

The more we learn about this jury, more unbelievable the feigned ignorance of current events and major political personalities appears, and the more inexorable and disturbing the conclusion that at least a couple of members of the Stone jury simply lied to the court in order to get themselves into the final twelve. (And that's before we get to the suspiciously similar answers many of them gave about their biases, which raises an even more horrifying specter—that several of them may have been coached.)

Perhaps not wishing to lie outright, two jurors simply didn't respond to this list of names. Naturally, both of the jurors who said they had some pre-existing opinions on politics nonetheless assured the court that they would be fair and impartial. Meanwhile, both listed the *New York Times* and the *Washington Post* as their primary trusted news sources.

Never mind the fact that some jurors listed as many as ten outlets from which they regularly consumed news, when asked about their opinions of Roger Stone or the Mueller investigation, *not a single juror admitted to having any specific opinion about Stone at all*. This, despite the wall-to-wall coverage at the end of the previous January of

Stone's paramilitary dawn raid arrest and the constant drumbeat from national and cable news about pending indictments.

Every juror save one claimed never to have posted anything on social media or a blog related to the Russia probe or the Mueller investigation. Tomeka Hart, somewhat comically, said she may have posted an article once or twice on Facebook but couldn't remember. We now know this was a bare-faced lie, under oath. Hart was posting negative tweets about Trump *while the trial was proceeding* and had mocked people who remarked on Roger Stone's excessive pre-dawn arrest.

One thing Hart might remember posting on Facebook is her all-smiles photo with Donna Brazile, former acting chair of the Democratic National Committee. And despite claiming not to pay close attention to the news, Hart has tweeted on multiple occasions about watching C.N.N. in the airport—even watching re-runs of the same show, which not even the show's hosts are guilty of.

Even more astonishingly, in sworn testimony, Hart claimed not to watch C-SPAN, which broadcasts proceedings of the federal government. But in a tweet, since discovered by reporters, to Rep. Diana DeGette, Democratic Congresswoman for Colorado's first district, she says the exact opposite. "Watching C-SPAN now. Thank you for being a voice of reason," she wrote. In other words, Hart lied under oath at least twice during the jury selection process.

On Twitter, Hart has referred to President Trump as a racist—which, despite its near-universal acceptance among liberals, is a completely unproven charge—and she once took time to praise the Mueller investigation, which was eventually to give rise to the selfsame Stone indictment with which this book is concerned, and for whom she was a foreperson in the jury.

Independent journalist Mike Cernovich was responsible for breaking the news that Tomeka Hart had a long trail of heavily partisan online commentary—one that also revealed a history of real-world activism, even including marches past Donald Trump's Washington, D.C. hotel. One Twitter post from August 2017 read: "Marched by 45's hotel…and the crowd went boooooo!!! Then yelled shame, shame, shame as we walked by!"

Hart celebrated the word "shithole" being projected on the outside wall of that hotel, and tweeted an article with the title, "What's so extremely, uniquely wrong about Trump's presidency." She even tweeted about the trial, using love heart emojis and a black fist emoji, on the day the jury voted to convict Stone on all counts, November 15, 2019, evidently celebrating her victory.

Hart, as recently as August 2019—a mere three months before the Stone trial—referred to all Trump supporters as racist, writing on Twitter: "Stop being racist. Co-signing and defending a racist and his racist rhetoric makes you racist. Point blank." She began to delete these tweets as they were pointed out by Cernovich and other journalists.

But it gets even worse. The article to which that tweet linked contained detailed information about Stone's indictment. This was information Hart would misunderstand, or at least later mis-state, in her jury questionnaire, but it gives the lie to any claim that she was not versed in the subject matter and completely biased from the start. It also makes a mockery of her feigned forgetfulness about whether or not she made posts about Mueller, Trump or Stone on social media ahead of the trial. She knows damn well that she did.

It stretches credulity to breaking point to imagine that a hyper-partisan political obsessive with her own electoral aspirations would have merely forgotten posting repeatedly about one of the most sensational news stories of the year. Judge Jackson, it should be noted, had all of this information at her fingertips when deciding whether or not to allow Hart to serve—including the fact that Hart referred to Trump on Facebook in 2017 as the "Klanpresident," in obvious reference to the Ku Klux Klan, and tweeted dozens, if not hundreds, of times about Mueller and Russia.

On Twitter, Hart can be seen tweeting about conference speakers "firing us up" to "act against the oppressive, racist agenda" of the Trump administration. Indeed, Hart was tweeting such detailed commentary about the attempt to impeach Donald Trump that she even posted notes to her followers about the correct application of the Latin phrase *quid pro quo*. To then claim she was able to serve as an impartial foreman for Roger Stone's criminal trial ought in itself to be a punishable crime—which, of course, it is.

Like Roger Stone, but for opposite reasons, Tomeka Hart will never see justice in Amy Berman Jackson's courtroom.

Mike Cernovich's verdict was simple. "The Roger Stone prosecution is a disgrace, it's lawless, and it was rigged from the beginning." It is difficult to disagree, especially when you consider that Tomeka Hart was merely one of twelve—perhaps the most egregiously and explicitly partisan, but by no means the only person wholly unfit to serve on the Stone jury.

Trump, too, had a few things to say, tweeting, "There has rarely been a juror so tainted as the forewoman in the Roger Stone case. Look at her background. She never revealed her hatred of 'Trump' and Stone. She was totally biased, as is the judge. Roger wasn't even working on my campaign. Miscarriage of justice. Sad to watch!"

Of the seven jurors who admitted to the court that they had heard something about the Stone case, each insisted they could only recall vague details and knew nothing of the specifics. In assuring the court of this peculiar, widespread outbreak of disinterest, the seven jurors used astonishingly similar language, including variations of the phrase "I didn't follow closely," which appears in six of the questionnaires.

What's really odd is that the jurors who claimed to be the most plugged in to the news, listing the most news sources, were the same jurors who maintained their complete ignorance about Roger Stone and insistence that they were totally personally indifferent to Stone, Trump and all the other names on the list. I'll leave that one as an exercise to the reader!

When you look more deeply into the backgrounds of the jurors, you discover information about their careers and family members that's even more disquieting than the obviously dishonest answers they give about their political affiliations, opinions and news consumption. Five of the twelve jurors were either lawyers, married to lawyers or had worked in law offices, several of which were state prosecutors, one of them in the same Washington, D.C. office bringing the case against Stone.

Six jurors out of twelve either worked for the federal government or were married to federal government employees, at agencies such as the I.R.S., the Department of Homeland Security and the T.S.A. Another worked for a university-based think tank. Two jurors had close connections to the F.B.I. One juror's father was a career recruiter for the C.I.A. Another juror's spouse was a key figure in the legal support team for the Senate Finance Committee.

Two different jurors had worked for Democrat Senators, and a third juror had worked for a Democrat in the House of Representatives. None had ever worked for a Republican. Even those who did not obviously or directly work for the government usually had roles related to public infrastructure or federal funding—with the politics to match. One city planner and "neighborhood advocate" runs a Twitter feed, which, again,

I am not identifying or quoting from directly out of respect for the juror's privacy, full of references to social justice themes, such as "L.G.B.T. representation" and race relations.

Most disturbingly of all, I have seen evidence that at least one juror's answers to the court were submitted in two completely different sets of handwriting, alternating in the course of a single document.

As for the jurors whose names are already known to the public, Tomeka Hart's jury questionnaire, widely available and freely passed around D.C. journalists during February 2020, shows clear evidence of outright dishonesty, as well as erroneous presumptions about the case. "Mr. Stone is accused of inappropriate contact [*sic*] Russian officials in the effort of helping Mr. Trump's campaign for President," she writes in response to a question about what Stone is on trial for. This is totally wrong. Stone was never accused of or indicted for contacting "Russian officials."

When asked about her social media activity related to the case, Hart writes: "I can't remember if I did, but I may have shared an article on Facebook. Honestly not sure." Like the other news junkies in the jury, she insists that any opinions she may hold "do not make it difficult for me to be fair" and that she only followed news reports about Stone "somewhat closely."

Hart, who is a lawyer and who ran for Congress as a Democrat in 2012—but insists she can be fair to Roger Stone—discloses that her cousin was murdered in 2011, for which no arrests were made, her niece was convicted of assault at her workplace in 2018, and is currently on probation, and her brother was recently arrested for drug possession and is now incarcerated.

Seth Cousins, the homosexual juror who donated $1,000 to Beto O'Rourke as recently as 2018, according to Federal Election Commission data, has also given to a number of other Left-wing causes, including ActBlue, a Democrat fundraising platform. True to gay form, he even gave money to Jill Stein—though only $250. Poor Jill. His online history shows many strident opinions in the obvious directions.

Maureen O'Leary, who was quoted swearing in the direction of Trump's White House by the *New York Times*, who listed such wildly Left-wing publications as *HuffPost* and *Buzzfeed* among the nine places she regularly read news online, and who cited Rachel Maddow, Anderson Cooper and Lawrence O'Donnell as her favorite three T.V. hosts, worked for A.B.C. and C.B.S. News before taking a job with the federal government. She insisted to the court that she had "no opinion" about Stone or the case.

How can it be, even in a place like Washington, D.C., that such an improbable cast of characters can represent a "random" selection of the public? How can it be that the jury gave such remarkably similar answers, in such remarkably similar language, to the same questions? The obvious answer is sickening to contemplate.

When, during the selection process, it came time to whittle down the pool to the final twelve, Stone's lawyers had to use their strikes to keep out former Clinton and

Obama employees, because Jackson had let them all in to the pool, in each case claiming that she trusted them to be impartial. So the defense team didn't get very far balancing out the jurors. The jury was overwhelmingly female, with just three men surviving to the final fourteen, which included two juror alternates in case of illness or indisposition.

Before I knew any of the information I later gathered for this book, sitting in the courtroom I couldn't identify a single working-class person—and certainly no one with a manual trade. (It turned out there was one.) As the awful reality began to sink in to Stone's supporters during jury selection, the tone of our conversations got darker. It felt hopeless.

It would only take one juror to see the injustice of what was happening and put a stop to it. But everything that could be done to engineer a guilty verdict had been done: The right judge had been locked in, the district was selected so as to be as hostile as possible, and the jury was hand-picked for the desired outcome. It was a classic stitch-up, as we say in England. A put-up job. And that's before we'd even heard from the witnesses.

CHAPTER FIVE: UNCLE STEVE

The Law matters throughout Western civilization, but it is especially cherished in, and central to, American public life. Courtrooms are the arena for America's great spiritual dramas, because the origin story of the United States depends on mythology that places the Law as sovereign over the King. Indeed, this is the whole reason America exists in the first place. From *Roe v. Wade* to the O.J. Simpson acquittal, legal arguments, spectacles, rituals and verdicts punctuate the Republic's evolving social attitudes and lay down examples for citizens follow. In a sense, trial verdicts are how America learns about itself. Court cases are sacred rituals where men are held to their word—and, of course, to statute.

At least, that's the theory. In reality, Washington, D.C., or the swamp, is a system of deliberate obfuscation and control. The swamp is the clutch of secrets the ruling classes keep to themselves—the arcane mysteries and rites of initiation that insulate the elites from the consequences of their actions, and preserve their power. Learning the ropes means learning how, for instance, to use procedural trickery to escape justice—or to lock in the judge you want.

When you have the full arsenal of the swamp at your disposal, you can nail anyone. Try to imagine if the F.B.I. got hold of every text and email you've ever sent, and whether or not they could, in the worst possible faith, construct an argument that you're a threatener, a brute and a barbarian and then hype up some ludicrous charge. Of course they could. With enough determination, time and resources—like the double-digit millions burned by the Mueller team—you can put just about anyone away, no matter how absurd or trivial the list of offenses.

On November 14, 2018, the *Daily Caller*'s Chuck Ross released a chain of documents that proved beyond doubt that Randy Credico was Roger Stone's source for information about the contents and timing of the WikiLeaks drop. "New text messages show that Roger Stone learned about WikiLeaks' plans to release Clinton-related emails through Randy Credico," wrote Ross. "The messages, which Stone's lawyers extracted from an old phone on Wednesday, back up Stone's claims about how he learned of WikiLeaks' plans. The messages severely undercut Credico's denials that he was a source for Stone."

"Credico has adamantly denied being Stone's con-duit," Ross continued, "Saying in numerous interviews over the past year that Stone was lying. Credico also told C.N.N. that his testimony to Mueller's grand jury on Sept. 7 was consistent with his public denials about being Stone's source. Pointing to the text messages, Stone asserts that Credico 'lied to the grand jury' if he indeed denied being Stone's contact to Assange." The Mueller grand jury had heard from two other sources, including filmmaker David Lugo, that Credico admitted to being Stone's point of contact.

And yet, at trial, the prosecution insisted that Credico was not Stone's source, once again trying to establish Stone as a prevaricator and a deceiver. Instead, prosecutors Kravis and Zelinsky pointed the finger at author Jerry Corsi, asserting that Corsi must have been Stone's source, but providing scant evidence for this claim. The only evidence the government could muster in fact undercut their own claims, such as an August 2 email exchange in which Corsi predicts, wrongly, that the WikiLeaks dump would come in August, and would contain information about the Clinton Foundation.

On October 3, Corsi texted Roger Stone: "Assange has nothing and has made a fool of himself." Hell of a prediction from the supposed middle man between Assange and Stone. The government didn't dare call Corsi as a witness. But let's take a look at who they did.

Precisely why the government thought it might be a good idea to introduce Trump's deputy campaign manager Rick Gates to the jury remains a mystery to all of us. Gates is a convicted felon who claimed at trial to have overheard a cell phone conversation about WikiLeaks between Stone and Trump while in an S.U.V. on the way to LaGuardia Airport in August of 2016.

In jumpy, halting testimony on the witness stand, an exhausted-looking Gates admitted he could not hear the words being spoken on the phone, and federal prosecutors produced no phone records nor any additional witnesses to corroborate the claim, even though there were two Secret Service agents in the vehicle at the time. The existence and contents of the call were assumed as fact by the prosecution. Both Trump and Stone deny that this conversation ever took place.

Rick Gates was convicted of conspiracy, and of lying to the F.B.I., but he served only forty-five days of his sentence in exchange for promising to testify against Stone. What's more, for his co-operation in the Stone trial and in Paul Manafort's, Gates was not prosecuted for an astonishing run of tax evasion on millions of dollars of income he admitted in court that he embezzled from his former partner Manafort, as part of his plea deal.

Nice fella, right? Stealing millions from his business partner and then ratting on the guy to send him to jail for seven and a half years. I don't envy his confessor priest. The point is, Gates is a rat. A jailhouse snitch. The kind of guy who will say literally anything to get himself out of a spot. Which begs the question: Why was he on the stand at all? His testimony isn't worth a damn.

I have one idea. The prosecution went a little long quizzing Gates about his crimes and his plea deal. I wondered if they were trying to kill their own witness, when it dawned on me why they wanted Bannon, an object of progressive loathing even rivalling the present author, and Gates, the obviously disreputable, sniveling wretch. It was to create a general spectacle of unsavory people all ratting on each other and dishing the dirt, so that Stone would be perceived as just another one of them—just another actor in the Trumpworld clown circus of liars, frauds and thieves.

Gates won't have to worry about dropping the soap like most jailhouse snitches, since he sold out to the feds to deliver Stone's head on a silver platter. A month and a half in jail. Even I could manage that, and perhaps even enjoy it.

Another way you know Gates was only there to taint Roger by association is that his claims on the stand were so hilariously weak. Gates claimed that Trump had taken a call from Roger Stone shortly before the WikiLeaks release, whereupon candidate Trump proclaimed to Gates that "another drop was coming soon."

No evidence exists of this phone call, and Julian Assange had already publicly announced that the focus of his upcoming releases was Hillary Clinton and the Clinton Foundation. It was the nothingest of nothingburgers. Federal prosecutors referred vaguely to emails they possessed which allegedly showed contact between Stone and Gates in the summer of 2016. Gates said Stone had asked him for contact information for Jared Kushner, the President's son-in-law. That has nothing to do with a phone call about WikiLeaks. But they could provide no further verisimilitude for Gates's claims beyond the fact that Gates and Stone had exchanged emails once.

More likely? Gates just made the whole thing up to establish as close a link as possible between Trump and Assange, the "Russian agent," to satisfy prosecutors. High school mock trials are conducted with higher evidence standards than this. And this is a pattern repeated in witness testimony throughout the Stone trial. The prosecution and Judge Jackson both claim that the charges against him were proven with documents alone. So why stage this he said-she said dog and pony show at all? Like I said, I think I know. Guilt by association with tainted and repugnant people.

We will never know how Rick Gates's testimony changed over the months he was hammering out a plea deal with the government, because any documents not under seal have been heavily redacted. We have no way of establishing his credibility beyond the obvious. That's just how the system works. First and foremost, it protects the government, so that whatever bribes, bullying, threats and backroom deals prosecutors strike to get their guy, the world can never know. If I knew for sure, and printed it, I'd be thrown in jail for contempt, just for telling you.

It's understandable that Gates would seek to escape a lengthy jail term by any moral means necessary. But that doesn't include making up lies about Roger Stone. And because, unlike some states which have transparency laws, the federal government is an opaque behemoth empowered to act without consequence, all we can do is speculate about how draconian the sentence that Weissman and pals dangled over Gates's head must have been, and how much of that Damocletian misery he bargained away with his fabrications.

* * *

Of all the characters impressionist, comedian and radio host Randy Credico performs, the most pitiable is Randy Credico. If you've ever heard someone describe a guy as having a punchable face, you're on your way to seeing Credico in your imagination. He has a rodent's small, black, darting eyes, set deep into a blotchy, weathered face that advertises a decades-long struggles with Schedule I (and II, IV and V) drugs. He's a drinker, too, with yellow teeth and thinning hair.

He gibbers, nervously, when he talks, weaving in and out of character so much that you never really know who you're looking at. He takes his glasses on and off. He plays with his hair. He mutters incomprehensibly. It's a strategy he's developed over the years. He's ashamed. He doesn't want you to look.

Credico and Stone's text messages, presented triumphantly by prosecutors, are not for the faint of heart. There's cocksuckers and fucks galore. But if you take your mind out of the urbane space in which it currently resides as you sip green tea, or maybe pressed juice, and read this elevated historiography, and think back to a time you heard your dad talk with his friends on the construction site, or—I don't know—the last time you had some plumbing work done, you'll begin to understand the milieu in which these two men exist: Bawdy, direct, macho and, yes, foul fucking mouthed. It is how working class men speak to one another when women aren't around.

For decades, Credico and Stone have been pals, despite their political differences. They enjoy the sort of vulgar and confrontational style that's so thrilling to watch in grown men who aren't afraid of their own physicality. It's not Sunday school. But it's also none of anybody else's business... until the F.B.I. gets a search warrant for your devices and decides that the ribald tone you employ privately actually represents a series of "threats" amounting to "witness intimidation."

Sometimes the overblown language between the two can be explicit, and graphic. But when the mainstream media claims that Randy Credico and his therapy dog, Bianca (no, really), were somehow targeted by Roger Stone, it is a lie—a lie perfectly packaged for T.V. and designed to create a particular sort of impression of Stone. Namely, that behind all the fancy suits and anecdotes about Nixon and Martinis with vermouth-marinated olives, he's really a thug and a bastard and he deserves to go away.

The truth is that Credico remains a drug addict and alcoholic, as three people confirmed to me in the course of writing this book. He may present as "saved" for public consumption, but he is as unstable, impressionable and unreliable as any other addict in the grip of compulsion.

Like many addicts, Credico can be charming, and even likeable, so he has been able to persuade the press quite easily that he is a victim of Stone's—as he did the jury, it seems.

When the emotionally fragile Credico says he felt "intimidated" by Stone, rocking backwards and forwards like a retarded child, it sounds plausible. Sure. But that excuses him from evasions and falsehoods he has since admitted to: Namely, that he led Stone on and misrepresented the extent of his contact with Assange. In other words, Stone could have been prosecuted for fibbing about a contact with WikiLeaks that might not even really have existed, unbeknownst to Stone, since Credico's bragging was, in his new telling of the story, mostly bravado and confection. It's all a felonious fable.

Credico did have a longstanding friendship with Margaret Kunstler, one of Assange's former lawyerrs. He denied this under oath in court, though it is a matter of public record and established fact. The extent to which Credico was scrambling, panicked, protecting his friends, or executing a premeditated deception can't be known. But anyone in that courtroom would have told you the same: Every word that comes out of this man's mouth is a lie, or sarcasm, or some new character he's come up with on the spot to avoid having to look you in the eye.

In the months before the trial, Credico had hurled himself onto any T.V. or radio show that would have him, crowing that Roger Stone was going to jail and whimpering about supposed threats to his dog, Bianca. When subpoenaed to testify, he showed up with Bianca in tow.

What you don't know, and what no one else will tell you, is that Credico abuses his dog by routinely failing to feed or care for her, in just the manner you'd expect from an addict. The dog sometimes goes days without food. If Stone's threat about snatching Bianca had been genuine, it would have been an act of humanitarian mercy.

When describing Credico's relationship with Stone, C.N.N. and M.S.N.B.C. used truncated or deceptively edited portions of their text message conversations to isolate colorful language by Stone and insulate Credico, in order to present him as the innocent victim of an unhinged mobster. Usually, they simply cut all of Credico's replies and showed a single message, shorn of all context, from Stone, usually including profanity.

On the stand, Stone's lawyer Robert Buschel got more truth out of Credico than the world had seen before. Credico admitted he did not think Stone—one of the most enthusiastic animal lovers in American politics—would ever actually harm Bianca. "He's a dog lover," admitted Credico on the stand. "I don't think he was going to steal my dog. I think he was pretty riled up at the time.... I know he wouldn't ever have touched that dog. It was hyperbole by him."

Credico has admitted on dozens of occasions in private conversations and even once on a movie set that he was Roger Stone's WikiLeaks "go-between," passing snippets of info to Stone on a regular basis about the timing and contents of new leaks. But more recently he has been spooked by the attention the Mueller investigation has brought anyone connected to Assange, and he now claims that this is not so. The text messages provided by Stone to the *Daily Caller*, however, do not lie—unlike federal prosecutors, who wrongly maintain that it was author Jerry Corsi giving Stone the heads-up.

Roger Stone even tried to protect Credico's identity, initially refusing to identify him to the House Intelligence Committee and only later doing so in writing. Once the cat was out of the bag, Stone, like everyone else, told Credico that the best way to keep himself out of jail and out of the spotlight was simply to shut up, and not talk to or co-operate with the F.B.I. Credico did not take this advice.

Credico, too, may have been threatened with jail time if he did not testify at Stone's trial. We know from other Mueller trials and other witnesses that such horse-trading was standard operating procedure for Weissman's team as they played Snakes and Ladders on the way to securing convictions of the Trump associates seen as bigger prizes, such as Manafort and Stone.

If I didn't know that's how he always is, I'd have assumed that Credico's extreme discomfort and constant fidgeting on the stand was evidence that he was betraying his conscience in throwing Stone to the wolves. Perhaps he needed a fix. Perhaps it was both.

As with all artificial highs, eventually the bill must be paid in regret and recriminations. The second Stone was convicted, Credico changed his tune. Realizing the enormity of his sins, he appealed at the eleventh hour to the judge not to give Stone a custodial sentence and said he never truly feared for his life. Who knows what the truth is? All that's for sure is that Randy Credico is not a credible witness, either in written private communications or on the stand. He's damaged goods. But even damaged goods will do when you're only staging a show trial, with a jury already lined up to convict.

To be found guilty of witness tampering with "enhancements" to the sentence added for threats, you don't need to prove that the target felt any pressure— only that there was intent to pervert justice. But even this standard was not satisfied in the Stone case, based on the clear, public written record between these men, which shows Stone as the senior partner in the friendship, sure, but definitely does *not* show a pattern of bullying, victimization, threats or abuse.

In order to believe that Stone was threatening Credico, you have to throw out every available speck of context. Or, to put it in plainer English, you have to lie.

* * *

Now for the deluxe. Steve Bannon, Trump's former chief strategist and my old boss. Thinking about my former mentor Bannon testifying, without subpoena, in the Stone case, I experienced the horror of watching a man I respected willfully damage a man I love. These two men have both been, in their own ways, father figures to me, though Bannon would probably scoff at the admission. So all this has felt like a kind of heartbreak. The former White House chief strategist, my superior during my infamous years as *Breitbart*'s main attraction and star writer, showed up to stick the knife into a political activist and showman who had become almost like family to me.

I have tried to figure out why Steve, who, for many years, I affectionately referred to as "uncle Steve," did it. I can't help but retain some admiration for a man I know to be preternaturally brilliant, well-read and foresighted. I can't overlook the fact that, many years after we were in the trenches together, Bannon refused in half a dozen interviews to disavow me, as so many other former friends and colleagues have done.

Even under aggressive questioning from the likes of the *Daily Beast*—a publication that has full-time members of staff tasked solely with whining about the social media feeds of popular conservative media figures— Bannon has always declined to distance himself from me, the young man he christened the "merry prankster" as we were plotting the torment of campus liberals half a decade ago. I can't ignore that entirely.

And yet there he was, in that courtroom in Washington, D.C.—absent a subpoena, it bears repeating—star witness in a trial he would under any other circumstances have been decrying from the sidelines as a witch hunt and a sham, dutifully giving the government lawyers what they wanted under the eye of a reproachful and fascinated jury, prattling and preening as Roger Stone's chance at freedom and justice withered.

It's Bannon's testimony that sealed count six, one of the counts of lying to the government, as well as a few others, probably. Stone had told the House Intelligence Committee that he never discussed his conversations with the person he referred to as "his intermediary" with anyone involved in the Trump campaign. "Both witnesses acknowledge getting updates from Mr. Stone," concluded Judge Jackson later, referring to Gates and Bannon. "They took him seriously, and they welcomed his particular brand of political assistance at a time the campaign needed all the help he could get."

But I've checked the court transcripts against my notes. Trump's former chief strategist Bannon, celebrated by the media as the government's star witness, contradicted himself a total of fourteen times on the witness stand. He first told the court, under direct examination by federal prosecutors, that Roger Stone had been the Trump campaign's "access point" to Wikileaks. But under cross-examination by Stone's lawyers, he denied it. Finally, Steve admitted the campaign had no "access point" to WikiLeaks at all, shattering the government's case against Stone. But, by then, the answers had been so many and so different that the jury was having trouble following what Bannon was really trying to say.

When Stone's lawyers sought to enter this muddled, contradictory sworn testimony before the House Intelligence Committee, prosecutors objected. And Judge Jackson, perhaps sensing that the star witness had not performed as well as expected and not wishing to further cast doubt on the one or two times Bannon had claimed

Stone was the campaign's WikiLeaks liaison, denied Stone's request to have Bannon's Permanent Select Committee testimony to be entered in as evidence in the case, which would have highlighted his shifting answers.

During his testimony, Bannon referred to Stone as an "agent provocateur," an "expert in opposition research," and an "expert in the tougher side of politics.... The types of things that campaigns use when they've got to make up some ground." It was testimony designed to repulse jury and judge and make Stone's work sound nefarious and illegal, and it worked. As *Rolling Stone* put it in a headline the following day: "Steve Bannon Threw Roger Stone Under The Bus At Trial."

I have personally been burned by loyalty to friends in the past, and even sometimes loyalty to passing acquaintances. Don't tell anyone, but I'm kind of a softie and tend to believe what people tell me. I hold personal loyalty above all other values. I try to abide by a code of honor. I confess I lack the cynicism of many people in journalism and politics, which might limit my successes. But I can sleep better than they can. I would not have made the same choice as Steve. They would have had to drag me there in manacles with a knife to my throat, assuring me of torture and death unless I co-operated, for me to say a word against a friend.

The most charitable explanation I can come up with for what I saw in Washington, D.C. is that Steve feels a loyalty, above and beyond fealty to any individual human being, to the refashioning of the United States to which he has dedicated so much of his life—in other words, that he believes that by saving himself, Steve Bannon, he is making the best strategic move for the future and for the country.

Fidelity can mean more than just sticking by your friends. It can mean fealty to principle and to nation— it can mean patriotism. Perhaps Steve thinks he has more left to give to the nation than Stone; perhaps he thinks he's better equipped to pursue the U.S.A.'s populist, nationalist future. If so, his particular brand of fidelity would mean he's occasionally disloyal to people but rarely untrue to principle. This would concord with the man I know, who thinks in world-historical terms and who has a justifiably high estimation of his own abilities and potential.

But I'm not convinced that this is a morally satisfactory answer. It's one thing to put principle over loyalty, but quite another to lie about an ally for the sake of principle.

It's true that Bannon and Stone have not always been fond of one another—and that most of the barbs have come from Stone. As recently as 2017, Stone was tweaking Bannon by including him in his annual "Worst Dressed" list, Bannon's third or fourth appearance on the list. Stone, I think, regards Bannon as a faux-messianic egotist; friends tell me Bannon views Stone with contempt as a a clownish almost-participant in the national drama. Both men, ridiculous in their own ways, always antagonistic and now locked in a fatal embrace, looked to me like the death of a nation: The elaborately mannered, mobster-suited master tactician undone by the slovenly but brilliant analyst and polymath.

I just can't forgive Steve. No glory as yet unrealized, no personal loathing, no relish in feuds concluded can justify the endorsement of, and participation in, this vile travesty. In the damp gloaming of a grim federal courthouse, seemingly for no reason at all, I watched my uncle Steve fade into a man I did not recognize, and did not care to know.

Maybe they had something huge on Bannon. Maybe they were threatening him. Honestly, I don't care. I'll never look at him and see uncle Steve again.

* * *

In November 2019, Roger Stone was found guilty of lying to Congress. The problem is, the Mueller investigation couldn't find any underlying crime for him to lie about. Prosecutors may have established at trial that Stone tried, without success, to learn the contents of forthcoming WikiLeaks disclosures. But that's not a crime. And it's certainly not evidence of collusion or conspiracy with Russia. In fact, throughout the trial, and then from Judge Jackson during sentencing, perfectly legal activities were cited as evidence of wrongdoing or stirred in gratuitously as verisimilitude in the assassination of Stone's character.

That's not surprising, because, for everyone involved in prosecuting Stone, it was all intensely political, and highly personal, from day one. Let me tell you about the people who brought the case in the first place. Overseeing Stone's case on behalf of the Special Counsel's office was Hillary Clinton intimate Jeannie Rhee. As I mentioned before, Rhee had represented Clinton in the small matter of Hillary's 33,000 deleted emails—while she was working in private practice at... Robert Mueller's old law firm.

She worked for Clinton throughout the period the former Secretary of State was found to have maintained a private server where classified documents were presumably received, stored, and sent. Then, Rhee was retained by the Clinton Foundation to defend against a racketeering lawsuit, before also being hired by Clinton advisor Ben Rhodes during the Benghazi investigation—the same investigation Amy Berman Jackson had protected Hillary from by refusing to hear a case from two sets of parents.

Rhee gave the maximum allowable contribution to Hillary's campaigns in 2008 and 2016, as well as donating to Obama in 2008. She cannot have been ignorant of the fact that Roger Stone was blistering about Clinton's mishandling of Benghazi, her illegal private email server, the mishandling of money at the Clinton Foundation and even her other client Ben Rhodes.

In fact, almost every political client Rhee represented within the span of a few short years was a target of Roger Stone's harsh public commentary. Yet Rhee did not recuse herself and instead took the reins of the Stone investigation, no doubt rubbing her flanks with glee at the prospect of revenge.

Aaron Zelinsky, Assistant U.S. Attorney and a former *HuffPost* blogger, was installed to assist Rhee in the Stone matter after urging by acting Attorney General Rod Rosenstein.

But the ultimate lead prosecutor, Assistant U.S. Attorney Johnathan Kravis, was… well, by now you probably won't be surprised by anything. He was Associate White House Counsel for President Barack Obama. A furious editorial in the *New York Times* about supposed "interference" in the Stone prosecution by Attorney General Bill Barr omitted to mention this fact—as it omitted to mention that the editorial's author, Bob Bauer, was Kravis's boss under Obama.

Completing the Stone prosecution team was the man who had successfully argued that an Act of Congress outlawing gay marriage was unconstitutional: Adam Jed. Jed was—yep, you guessed it—also an Obama-era employee, this time from the Department of Justice, who had worked on the Gates and Manafort cases and who had in the past defended Obamacare in court.

Of the remaining investigators and prosecutors, of which there were nearly two dozen in some fashion involved with the Stone case, almost every one of them had some kind of connection to a Democrat politician or a political donation history that ought to have disqualified them from serving. No one recused themselves.

This is what people mean when they talk about the

swamp of Washington, D.C., and the casual indifference to due process that's possible when you are a member of the ruling elite, and you know that there are no consequences for your bad behavior, and that no matter what you do, provided you have the right political enemies, you will be protected by other members of the Leftist establishment.

As of this writing, House Republicans are calling for an investigation into several of the Stone prosecutors, though their alleged offenses relate to the earlier Flynn and Papadopoulos cases. But none of the aforementioned swamp creatures comes close to the ugly specter of Andrew Weissman, a lead on the Mueller investigation who made his name grilling the Chief Financial Officer of Enron with a barely-legal blend of interrogation and wild threats.

Weissman's handling of the Enron investigation cost thousands of Americans their jobs, and his convictions were later overturned by the Supreme Court by unanimous vote. He should have been disbarred long ago, but he has been allowed to amass power in Washington, D.C. A top donor to the Obama Victory Fund, the Democratic National Committee and the Clinton presidential campaigns, Weissman has used his position to punish and persecute Republicans with sadistic promises of endless grand jury investigations and threats of indictments.

When the four lead prosecutors on Stone's case quit after Attorney General Bill Barr smacked down their outrageous sentencing memo—that's a letter prosecutors write to a judge in which they ask for a particular custodial sentence, or lack thereof, and which the Stone prosecutors used to recommend a grotesque nine-year sentence—the case temporarily fell to J.P. Cooney, the Department of Justice's head of fraud and corruption as the lead on Stone.

But even Cooney had a history that should have disqualified him. Cooney authored a D.O.J. memo recommending that leaker and liar Andrew McCabe should not be prosecuted, even though McCabe is alleged to have committed crimes remarkably similar to those of which Roger Stone was accused.

This is not justice. And it's a grisly sight, watching Trump's Justice Department hunting down and jailing his associates while letting contemptible swamp creatures off the hook. Congressional Republicans have adopted the same "wait and see" approach as the President, so they've been no use either. Was it really too much to ask for them to throw a bone to Stone, who helped get their man into the White House?

∗ ∗ ∗

There is no doubt about it: Roger Stone was selectively prosecuted by dyed-in-the-wool partisan political opponents, and treated like a violent fugitive, rather than a political operative of pensionable age. When you look back at the decades of Stone's political activities, you find links and contextual clues about why this case was brought, and how it was done. In short, Stone has been so good at his job that he has amassed thousands of enemies in the deep state and on the Democratic side without even knowing it.

Recall that in 2015, Roger Stone published *The Clintons' War on Women*, a savage account of not only Bill Clinton's serial sexual assaults, but also, and more damningly, Hillary's role in intimidating, bullying and silencing Bill's victims. What's more, Stone was the first person to draw attention to Bill Clinton's connection with pedophile Jeffrey Epstein: *The Clintons' War on Women* documented Bill's twenty-eight flights to Epstein's private island, and Epstein's role in the founding of the Clinton Foundation. After all this, we are expected to believe that Jeannie Rhee's close relationship with the Clintons had no effect on her prosecutorial decision-making with respect to Stone.

This bias revealed itself in the absurdity of the statements made during trial, and the eventual conviction, especially in the outlandish interpretations of Stone's behavior. For instance, Stone was charged and convicted under the False Statements Act, which requires not only that a statement be false, but also that it be material and that there should exist "an intent to deceive." The prosecution, in its closing arguments, said Stone lied to Congress about Russia and WikiLeaks because "the truth wouldn't look good for Donald Trump." That's the only reason they gave for Stone's actions—the only basis on which to convict.

Judge Jackson repeated this prosecutorial narrative during sentencing. "Whether Stone was ever actually in communication with Assange or not, he understood full well that it could reflect badly on the President if someone learned that he'd exchanged emails ... about what Assange was about to do or that he'd sent messages trying to get Assange to release emails on a particular topic on a particular schedule, or that there were emails between himself and Bannon, Gates, and Manafort as he reported in on all of this to the campaign," she claimed.

This is, quite simply, bonkers. Candidate Trump spoke openly about his and his campaign's interest in the WikiLeaks materials. In October 2016 in Pennsylvania, Trump said: "This just came out. WikiLeaks, I love WikiLeaks." Two days later, in Ocala, Florida, Trump told the crowd: "This WikiLeaks stuff is unbelievable. It tells you the inner heart. You gotta read it." A day after that, in Ohio, the candidate said: "It's been amazing what's coming out on WikiLeaks."

At the end of October, in Michigan, Trump proclaimed: "Another one came in today. This WikiLeaks is like a treasure trove." And in November, back in Ohio again, Donald Trump told his supporters: "Getting off the plane, they were just announcing new WikiLeaks, and I wanted to stay there, but I didn't want to keep you waiting. Boy, I love reading those WikiLeaks."

According to M.S.N.B.C., Trump mentioned WikiLeaks no fewer than 141 times in the month before the 2016 election. So to what end would Stone conceivably be lying about the President's interest in the disclosures? It was there for all to see, coming out of the candidate's mouth on a near-nightly basis. Stone, testifying voluntarily and without subpoena, had no motive to dissemble about legal, legitimate political activity. But prosecutors said he had an intent to deceive—and the jury went along with it.

And prosecutors went way further than the House Intelligence Committee itself in apportioning blame to Roger Stone. The Committee voted to turn over Stone's classified testimony at Robert Mueller's request, but they did not refer Stone for prosecution and the Committee's final report did not find that Stone has misled them. Even at trial, there was no testimony or evidence that the Trump team had learned anything about WikiLeaks, or that Stone had shared with the Trump campaign team any information, that was not public on Stone's Twitter feed.

As for the comically inflated charge of witness tampering, Stone had already told the House Intelligence Committee that Randy Credico was his source about the timing and contents of WikiLeaks disclosures. Stone and Credico had worked together before on criminal justice reform. Stone urged Credico to assert his Fifth Amendment right not to testify before the House not to protect Stone, but because Credico said he feared the public opprobrium that might come if it became public that he had, in some way, "helped Trump." A number of reporters, the A.C.L.U. and Credico's own lawyer gave the radio host the exact same advice.

What Roger Stone was punished for in Amy Berman Jackson's courtroom was, at least partly, being flamboyant and colorful. Because the phrasing, sometimes funny, sometimes aggressive, sometimes referring to popular culture, did not fit within the ordinary understanding and communications patterns of drably dressed and even more drably spoken judges and government lawyers—because he likes to cuss, and because he has chosen to cultivate an image of dangerous unpredictability—Stone's texts and emails were misrepresented as evidence of criminal intent.

Is it some kind of female equivalent of small man's syndrome, this violent hatred of the polished, the self-confident and the stylish? The irrational loathing those of us with cheekbones receive from plain-looking women in positions of power is one of life's great mysteries, and one of the dozens of disadvantages popular, athletic, handsome men have to contend with these days.

More likely is that, as with so much in the Trump era, what this all really boils down to is class. The uptight, thin-lipped attitudes of the D.C. elites are horrified by the way ordinary people think and speak.

On January 20, 2020, Randy Credico wrote a letter to Judge Jackson begging for leniency for Stone and affirming that he never felt threatened. Credico asked the judge not to send Stone to jail. These are remarkable actions for someone supposedly intimidated, tampered with and who was afraid that his dog was going to be stolen or killed, one of the well-lubricated, overheated late-night Stone texts, that prosecutors had pretended at trial represented a sincere threat.

A month later, Judge Jackson would prove to be unimpressed: "It's nice that Mr. Credico has forgiven Stone ... but all that says more about Mr. Credico than

Stone.... He also appeared on the stand to be a highly nervous individual. And it may well be that, even today, he just doesn't want to be known as the reason behind a tough sentence."

It's easy to feel sorry for Credico, who cut a pathetic figure in court, as he does in life. Especially when, in perhaps the most entertaining part of the trial, the prosecution revealed that Stone had doctored a version of his letter naming Credico as the WikiLeaks intermediary, adding cloying praise and paragraphs of obsequious flattery. He sent that copy to Credico, telling Credico it was the letter he'd submitted to Congress, when in fact his letter to Congress had been considerably more ambivalent.

Your mileage, dear reader, is going to vary on this one. Those of us who relish intrigue, drama and a little light manipulation see it as a gloriously Machiavellian move by Stone—one that would never have come to light were it not for the F.B.I. and the Mueller investigation. But you might be gasping in horror at its wickedness. If so, I recommend that you avoid a career in politics.

CHAPTER SIX: BLOOD FROM A STONE

"If anybody in this room has sunglasses on, unless there's a medical reason, they need to take them off." Believe it or not, Judge Jackson wasn't talking to me, but rather a photosensitive Stone supporter. But I was asked to step outside once or twice for nodding off in the stifling courtroom atmosphere, as were half a dozen others.

They must do it on purpose to punish those of us with air conditioning at home. One young podcaster, Chris Cella, was forcibly removed from the overflow room and physically ejected from the building for groaning during Jackson's sentencing remarks, as the judge heaped moral condemnation on Stone's character and conduct.

"Roger Stone will not be sentenced for who his friends are or for who his enemies are," claimed Judge Jackson, pausing as if to check for incredulous titters. "He's not going to be sentenced for his reputation or his personality or his work. The record doesn't begin to enable me to figure out which supposed dirty tricks he actually committed and which he just took credit for, and it doesn't matter."

But that statement is belied by Jackson's own withering attitude to Stone, made clear not only by her own conduct during the trial but by her contemptuous remarks while delivering the selfsame sentence, and the relish with which she quoted Randy Credico's assessment of Stone's character. "Stone enjoys playing adolescent mind games and pulling off juvenile stunts, gags, pranks. He shamelessly invents and promotes outlandish and invidious conspiracy tails. But the bottom line is, Mr. Stone, at his core, is an insecure person who craves and recklessly pursues attention."

It's belied when she adds her own earnest summary to Credico's vicious observation. "The problem is that nothing about this case was a joke; it wasn't funny, it wasn't a stunt, and it wasn't a prank. Stone's conduct displayed flagrant disrespect for the institution of government established by the Constitution, including Congress and this Court. And I'll venture to say that even many adolescents know the difference."

It's belied when she in effect rebuked Stone for the overheated commentary of his friend and erstwhile employer, Alex Jones, over which Stone had no control: "The host of *InfoWars*, Alex Jones,... began publishing incendiary and false information about the composition of the jury beginning on November 5th, the first day of *voir dire*."

And it's belied by Jackson when she echoes smug *Washington Post* talking points about Trump and the 2016 election to intone: "The truth still exists. The truth still matters. Roger Stone's insistence that it doesn't, his belligerence, his pride in his own lies are a threat to our most fundamental institutions, to the very foundation of our democracy."

"The judge in the Roger Stone case is showing the world how trials are conducted every day," commented Mike Cernovich, who is also a lawyer, upon hearing these remarks. "This isn't limited to Roger Stone. Federal judges straight don't give a F*CK about due process. They are prosecutors in black robes."

As we sat and listened to Judge Amy Berman Jackson warm to her theme in that stifling courtroom on February 20, 2020, the full horror and reality dawned on us of Jackson's ability and clear intent to have Roger spend his final days in jail. On count after count, the obvious, common-sense explanation of events was rejected by Jackson in favor of the government's eccentric claims. She also repeated many of the government's entirely false assertions.

"The evidence included numerous written communications, including emails and texts in which the defendant repeatedly urged Mr. Credico to assert his Fifth Amendment privilege against self-incrimination, to claim a failure of recollection, to 'do a Frank Pentangeli,' a shared reference to *The Godfather* that Credico immediately understood to mean feign a lack of knowledge, or to straight out lie, all to support the false narrative advanced by Stone, that Credico had been an intermediary between Stone and Julian Assange, to whom Stone publicly referred in early August of 2016," declared Jackson, despite the fact that Stone had presented text messages establishing beyond doubt that Credico was Stone's intermediary to WikiLeaks.

Again and again, Jackson chose to join prosecutors in interpreting the comic overstatement of two men launching barbs at one another as evidence of sincere threats to do harm. "I'm going to take that dog away from you. Not a fucking thing you can do about it either because you are a weak, broke piece of shit. I will prove to the world that you are a liar," Stone had written to Credico, before adding, as if to underscore the theatricality of the exchange: "I'm so ready. Let's get it on. Prepare to die, cocksucker."

"Defendant's memorandum refers to this as banter, which it hardly is," was Jackson's po-faced conclusion.

∗ ∗ ∗

I hope I don't ever get into serious trouble and need their help, because I have to say it: Roger Stone deserved a better legal team. Although, in truth, he could have had every private practice lawyer in America in that room and it wouldn't have made much of a difference with Judge Jackson in the chair and Tomeka Hart running the jury. I'll get in trouble with friends for saying this, but I have to wonder whether Bruce Rogow, the renowned First Amendment lawyer who has argued countless landmark cases before the Supreme Court, has seen better days.

Rogow has notched some impressive victories in his career, and has an impeccable reputation, but set against the blood-crazed ferrets of the prosecution team his approach lacked the necessary vim and vigor to provide a persuasive defense. I could see the jury checking their watches and doodling when Rogow was speaking, which they didn't while Kravis and Zelinsky brandished flow charts, rattled off dates and data points into mics and generally brought a sense of urgency to proceedings. Rogow seemed tired—the opposite of what an underdog defense team needs.

Robert Buschell, another of Stone's attorneys, presented well on paper, with a background as a criminal defense lawyer and case histories running the gamut from corruption to white-collar infractions. But a bulldog this former public defender is not. Like Rogow, I had to reluctantly conclude that there was a spark missing with Buschell that might have made the odd juror sit up and take notice. Neither of them seemed willing or able to push back on Jackson's alternate-dimension decisions. And neither of them apparently did much research on the jurors, because they completely missed Tomeka Hart, who would have been anyone's first strike given the contents of her public Twitter and Facebook feeds.

* * *

In the weeks leading up to Roger Stone's sentencing, we were not hopeful. Rumor had it the prosecution was going to ask for as many as ten years in the sentencing memo, with the consensus being that Judge Jackson would settle somewhere around six to eight years, with possible enhancements. Enhancements are like upgrades or, for those of you who play video games, power-ups. So, for instance, if you tampered with a witness and also threatened their property or, for instance a dog, even jokingly, a judge might decide to tack a little bit extra on for the added seriousness, or added premeditation, or added whatever.

Before sentencing, Stone added a more aggressive defensive component to the mix: Seth Ginsberg, a New York City attorney best known for representing the Gotti and Lucchese crime families. Hot, right? Ginsberg brought some clout and brashness, and even Jackson seemed to negotiate with him differently than she had the previous two advocates. But, by then, we were down to bargaining over a few more months in jail. The horse had already bolted.

Stone allies muttered darkly about Stone being Ep-steined in jail as revenge for 2016. It sounded stupid—why would he be?—but then someone pointed out that Stone's aggressive public relations effort getting the story of Bill Clinton's estranged and abandoned black son Danney Williams in front of African-American voters had been instrumental in key swing states. Black voters hadn't turned out *en masse* for Trump, but they hadn't felt able to vote for Hillary either, and that was good enough.

It would only take a couple of days inside for something to be arranged.

We'd seen enough from Jackson to know that Stone was going to get the maximum sentence she could get away with handing down, without providing grounds for an appeal or attracting criticism from her peers. Maybe she wouldn't order the dirt nap herself. But she'd make sure Stone was in jail for plenty of time. Jackson brushed off concerns about bias, concerns about the jury and every other objection Stone's counsel made.

The shocking news that the prosecution had indeed requested anything up to nine years' incarceration handed the Stone team back the advantage, at least in the public mind. It was a ludicrous, astonishing, outrageous recommendation. Even establishment Republicans who loathed Stone said so. A nine-year prison sentence for a sixty-seven year old man, even one in good shape, is the same as a life sentence. Older inmates can deteriorate rapidly given the conditions in federal prisons, which is why allowances are usually made when a defendant is older, non-violent and a first-time offender. And all Trump had done—even if you took the view that he was guilty—was prevaricate to Adam Schiff.

Proseuctors Kravis and Zelinsky, drunk on victory, it's said—accounts differ—didn't bother to run their sentencing recommendation up the flagpole before submitting it to the court. They probably assumed Jackson would give them whatever they wanted. But they didn't count on the public outcry. In a rare moment of unity, conservatives and moderates up and down the country expressed indignation at the sociopathic cruelty of the prosecutorial team, and sympathy for Stone.

The sentencing memo reiterated dozens of easily disproved falsehoods about Stone amid heavily over-egged and apocalyptic warnings about the danger he supposedly posed to American democracy, and asked for a sentence that was unprecedented in length. Fortunately, senior figures in the Justice Department put an almost immediate halt to it. The shock prompted Trump to start tweeting regularly about Stone, which continued throughout sentencing, perhaps not always to Stone's benefit. But, he called it "disgraceful" and a "miscarriage of justice," which it obviously was.

Attorney General Bill Barr stood by news reports in which Justice officials claimed they were ill-informed and implied they were lied to or simply not briefed at all by the prosecutors. When the Justice Department announced that it would be revising its recommendation down, all four prosecutors threw a temper tantrum and withdrew from the case in protest, with Kravis even resigning entirely from his job.

Jury foreman and lawyer Tomeka Hart felt sufficiently emboldened to out herself on Facebook in a long post supporting the prosecutors, which is how her name came to be public information, and why we can reveal it in this book. "I want to stand up for Aaron Zelinsky, Adam Jed, Michael Marando, and Jonathan Kravis— the prosecutors on the Roger Stone trial," Hart wrote. "It pains me to see the D.O.J. now interfere with the hard work of the prosecutors. They acted with the utmost intelligence, integrity, and respect for our system of justice."

Helpfully confirming the suspicion among Stone allies and the Trump movement more generally that we are up against a highly organized and well co-ordinated Left-wing bureaucracy that swings into action to protect its own with terrifying speed and power, 1,100 former Justice Department employees signed a letter condemning Bill Barr within just twenty-four hours. Imagine trying to get 1,100 Republicans to do *anything* together in twenty-four hours.

President Trump continued to tweet about the injustice. Former New York City Mayor Rudy Giuliani, constitutional law expert Alan Dershowitz, and libertarian legal hawk Judge Andrew Napolitano all issued strong rebukes against the sentencing memo. They even argued that the discovery of Hart's bias was enough to push for a mistrial and presented a strong case for a presidential pardon.

The Justice Department quickly issued a new recommendation of three to four years for Stone, while mainstream cable news hosts wailed about "interference" from Barr and Trump. Tucker Carlson, who at this stage had been pushing for a pardon of Roger Stone for weeks, used his primetime program to deliver impassioned pleas to the White House for clemency, knowing that Trump takes his opinion seriously as a bellwether of his core voting base.

When Stone's lawyers moved to have Judge Jackson recuse herself, alleging bias, the threat of losing her grip on the trial prompted a speedy and irritated response from the judge, who, in a flabbergasting display of *chutzpah*, accused the defense of abusing the court's docket with its claims of bias. "Judges cannot be 'biased' and need not be disqualified if the views they express are based on what they learned while doing the job they were appointed to do," she wrote. So that's the end of that.

One thing had become clear in these final days before Stone would learn his fate. Public pressure had to be placed on the prosecutors and judge. They could not stand criticism or scrutiny of their decisions. They had spent a career unchecked, never held to account. Supporters of Stone had two equally important tasks: Push President Trump for a presidential pardon, and make sure the entire nation knew what had gone down during this rigged trial.

Stone formally requested a new trial, given all that had happened, in the early morning hours of Valentine's Day, February 14, 2020, just six days before he was due to be sentenced. As this book goes to print, Jackson is yet to rule on the motion. But Stone and his lawyers aren't holding their breath.

* * *

In the first two pages of Roger Stone's federal indictment, an underlying premise is stated: That Russians hacked the Democratic National Committee and provided the information they obtained to Julian Assange and WikiLeaks. Every "lie" that Stone was supposedly caught in rests upon this alleged, but as yet unproven, action. And the way you know that even Stone's political opponents aren't sure about it is their own selective approach to its veracity and practical application.

Amy Berman Jackson would not allow Roger Stone's lawyers to disprove the allegation upon which every charge made against him rested. She would not allow Stone to call forensic witnesses such as Bill Binney, a former National Security Agency intelligence official and whistleblower. Stone's entire prosecution is based on this fundamental assumption—but when it came to evidence and witnesses, federal prosecutors suddenly decided that its truth or falsehood was irrelevant to the facts of whether or not Stone lied. Judge Jackson let them get away with it.

And there was another, curious episode, during the discovery phase of the case. While the body of evidence for the trial was being agreed upon, the government reluctantly admitted that the F.B.I. had never directly inspected the D.N.C.'s computer servers—an almost unprecedented step—and had instead relied, if you recall, on that "redacted draft memo" from Clinton-linked I.T. firm CrowdStrike. This admission attracted broad media coverage, because it was so unusual.

Somewhere, within the bowels of the deep state, a klaxon went off, and so, the very next day, the government filed a "sur-reply," amending its previous statement and claiming that prosecutors did in fact have additional evidence, beyond the CrowdStrike memo, that the Russians had been responsible for the hack. But they gave no indication of what that evidence might be. There was no proof.

To this day, as far as the world knows, the Federal Bureau of Investigation took on trust a one-page, part-redacted summary memo from a firm closely tied to Hillary Clinton, and performed no first-hand forensic investigation of its own whatsoever.

If this is true, it is unprecedented in the history of the Bureau, given the extraordinary seriousness and profile of the alleged hack. You would think that the F.B.I. would want to reassure the public, and protect its own reputation, by explaining why it was so confident that Russians were responsible. But it hasn't, perhaps because it can't. So we are left with the claim, absent any proof at all, that it just so happened to be the same sinister Russians at whom the Democrats were pointing fingers throughout the election, who also hacked the D.N.C., giving a much-needed boost to the Trump campaign.

A key line of defense for Stone was, of course, that he had been prosecuted selectively and that prosecutors and members of Congress had acted improperly in the run up to the indictment. This is a respectable and well-trodden defense strategy. But, perhaps because this was such a powerful line of argument, and because, unlike the government, Stone could back up his assertions, Judge Jackson said no. "There will be no investigating of the investigators in my courtroom," she told lawyers

Wrongdoing and dishonest, disreputable and possibly illegal behavior by the people bringing charges against

Stone is critical contextual information, demonstrating that Stone's trial was politically-motivated and his prosecution was selective and had nothing to do with Russia. The jury ought to have been provided with this context and asked to consider why American taxpayers' money was spent hunting down errors and technicalities to put friends and associates of Donald Trump behind bars by the same Democrat-voting state apparatus that tried so hard to thwart the 2016 election.

Stone's lawyers were barred from raising any questions about the misconduct, or bias, of the Special Prosecutor, the Department of Justice, the F.B.I. or any Members of Congress, despite the fact that Attorney General Bill Barr had appointed Special Counsel John Durham to investigate precisely that. Since there's no case that prosecutorial misconduct is irrelevant, and clearly even the United States Attorney General thinks something was up, it's impossible to understand Judge Jackson's ruling as anything other than interference in the defense. Once again, Amy Berman Jackson had identified a key plank of the defense strategy ahead of time and smashed it into pieces.

We don't have to wait for the outcome of John Durham's investigation to know if Members of Congress acted improperly with respect to Stone. Congressman Adam Schiff admitted that he co-ordinated with the Office of the Special Counsel, in violation of House Rules, in a letter to Intelligence Committee Chairman Devin Nunes. This was presented to Judge Jackson during the trial. She forbade Stone's lawyers from bringing it up, despite clear indications that the prosecution was a set-up from the beginning.

That's not all Schiff did. According to the *Washington Post*, Robert Mueller had an advance copy of Stone's classified testimony—another violation of House rules—before the Committee had voted to release it to him. No investigation has been made of this and no charges brought. It was impossible for Congressman Schiff and his colleagues Eric Swalwell and Joaquin Castro to know, without having seen the results of surveillance on Roger Stone, whether he might face criminal charges. But all three of them predicted immediately after Stone's Congressional testimony that he would be indicted for perjury, suggesting that the entire hearing was one long exercise in dishonesty, entrapment and partisan warfare.

CHAPTER SEVEN: MISTER PRESIDENT

Roger Stone's Fifth Amendment right to a fair and impartial trial was destroyed the moment federal prosecutors locked in Amy Berman Jackson as judge. Jackson did everything she could to hog-tie and hamstring the defense, ruling against Stone's lawyers again and again, on matters both trivial and substantial.

His Sixth Amendment right to an impartial jury was also, as this book has shown, violated repeatedly by the stacking of a Washington, D.C. jury that wasn't only politically biased—it's doubtful any Republican could get a fair trial in D.C.—but was in fact crafted, hand-selected and packed full of Democrat lawyers, Democratic Capitol Hill employees and Democrat political operatives.

You could persuasively argue that Stone's Fourth Amendment right against baseless search and seizure had been infringed, too, given the illegal surveillance he has been subjected to since at least 2016. But Judge Jackson didn't stop there—not when there were more Amendments left to infringe.

If you're wondering why you haven't heard much from Roger Stone since he was arraigned, that's not because the loquacious author has lost any of his showiness or bombast. Rather, Stone was gagged—and not in the fashion he might have enjoyed in the 1990s. Even post-conviction and, as the book you're reading went to press, even *post-sentencing*, Stone has been forbidden from discussing his trial in public, denied the right to clear his name.

Stone hasn't commented in public or in private on the trial—not to me, not to our rambunctious mutual buddy Alex Jones, not to anyone—though that hasn't stopped prosecutors and Judge Jackson aggressively searching for infractions with which to punish him throughout the process. What little we know has been gleaned from family members and friends.

Stone's wife, Nydia, finally confirmed what a lot of us were privately suspecting when she revealed that her husband was prosecuted because he refused a deal to falsely testify against President Trump about the contents of some twenty-five phone calls between the pair in 2016. Presumably, prosecutors wanted Stone to say that Trump was orchestrating or in some other way directly involved with Julian Assange to construct a case for Russian collusion. Stone said No—so he got the rope.

Why were Roger Stone's First Amendment rights suspended in such an extraordinary fashion, and why does he remain unable to defend himself? The rationale for Stone's original gag order, according to Judge Jackson, was that his regular and vigorous public self-defense in the media might taint the jury pool. The *Washington Post*, C.N.N., M.S.N.B.C., N.B.C., C.B.S., the *New York Times*, the *Daily Beast*, *Vox*, *Vice* and others have, for two years now, steadily fed the public a series of leaks from the Mueller investigation designed to incriminate its targets in the public imagination, and another series of leaks designed to leave the impression that Stone would be prosecuted for treason and conspiracy against the United States—and that he was the link between the Trump campaign and Russia.

All of this is wholly false, but it is a narrative that was maintained constantly by the press. As we now know, the outlets leading the charge were precisely those the Stone jury was most regularly reading and watching. Judge Jackson's contention is that Stone's interviews and his show on *InfoWars* might contaminate the jury in a way that the combined might of the American media establishment—*i.e.*, the shows the jurors actually watched—would not.

Perhaps getting wind of the bad press this gag order was receiving, Amy Berman Jackson addressed her constitutionally dubious instructions in February 2020: "[Stone's] record of travel belies the narrative being disseminated that I silenced him or took away his ability to speak or to earn a living. When the case began, there were no restrictions on Mr. Stone at all. After he posted an incendiary, threatening post regarding the Court, I took the suggestion of the defendant's own First Amendment lawyer and barred him from making comments about this case, but that was all.

"He couldn't obey that either. When he was still on bond, he continued to post about others involved in the investigation, and that led to the requirement that he not Tweet or post or use Instagram. He withdrew his own appeal of that condition, and he didn't even ask to be relieved of it pending sentence. But there has never been a prohibition on his writing, giving a speech and getting paid for it, or any other means of earning a living."

At the risk of ticking off a federal judge: What a load of old bollocks.

*** * ***

The Special Counsel system urgently needs wholesale reform. No longer should the American taxpayer be expected to pay tens of millions of dollars for one party to attack elected officials, and their friends and allies, in the other party. It's wrong. It's sick. And it is destroying the lives of innocent people who find themselves on the wrong side of the electoral equation.

Simple but urgently needed reform of the Special Counsel system, to avoid the abuses to which the Mueller report gave rise, should look something like this. Firstly, if the primary areas of investigation prove fruitless, there can be no concomitant crimes. What I mean is: You can't prosecute someone for obstruction of an investigation when the investigation finds that no initial crime was committed. Innocent men should be completely protected from the consequences of attempting to prove their innocence.

Secondly, Special Counsels should lose the power to hand down indictments for crimes unrelated to the scope and parameters of their investigation, to avoid the sort of specious trials and politically-motivated wrongdoing from the feds that have characterized the Stone case. Exceptions could be made for very serious crimes. If, in the course of their investigations, Special Counsels discover evidence of a capital crime or some other substantial and serious offense, such as treason, then fine.

But granting Special Counsels *carte blanche* to indict anyone who's ever met anyone who's ever worked for the subject of the investigation for whatever they can find is an invitation to obscene abuses of power, and it has to stop. If a Special Counsel is appointed to investigate whether a President or someone on his campaign team colluded with Russia to steal an election, then that is the scope within which the indictments have to sit.

Otherwise, look forward to a grim future in which each party takes turns destroying the reputations and livelihoods of every future sitting President as revenge for losing a free and fair election. This, of course, has an electoral dimension that no one bringing the charges has missed: If you lock up a President's entire electoral team, you weaken his changes the next time around, because when he runs for re-election, all his first picks for staff are locked up.

Special Counsels should be focused on securing criminal prosecutions, which should not be undertaken unless it's clear that the subject of the investigation has broken the criminal law. This would dramatically reduce the number of prosecutions and ensure that prosecutions are restricted to serious matters within the scope of the initial investigation.

The Special Counsel should also have its prosecutorial role de-emphasized and instead a focus should be placed on accountability: in other words, on its detailed reporting. This way, the public is more fully informed about the facts and context of the investigation's subject matter, and the Department of Justice can decide whether to bring further prosecutions based on facts that clearly support a criminal conviction.

In most cases, it will be the public's job to make up their minds about wrongdoing and punish a President or other senior official at the ballot box, or via their elected representatives using the clear, unambiguous and constitutionally-defined impeachment process.

Finally, it wouldn't be a terrible idea if the team appointed by the Special Prosecutor were, you know, not united in contempt and hatred for the subject of their investigation and everyone around him. I'll leave it to someone else to come up with a plan for that one, but it seems reasonable to introduce new and much stricter rules about who can join prosecutorial teams—namely, you can't serve in the White House of one party and then prosecute people from the other. Radical, I know.

∗ ∗ ∗

Roger Stone, the final victim of the Mueller witch hunt, was railroaded by a politically biased judge and a stacked jury. He has been sentenced to three-and-a-half years in jail, which, despite his rude health, could be the same thing as a life sentence. He has been bankrupted by the costs of this trial, which his lawyers estimate could eventually run to $3 million. The Stone family have lost their home, their savings, and even their health insurance. Nydia Stone is now 71. She is almost completely without hearing and has no means of supporting herself if her husband is incarcerated. Nothing, not even a presidential pardon, will undo the financial ruin Stone has suffered for refusing to roll on his friend, Donald J. Trump.

Although 200,000 Americans have signed one of the online petitions to free Roger Stone so far, and although Trump himself has correctly branded the Stone trial a "hoax," no pardon has come from the White House, nor even a commutation of the sentence, which, surely, is the least Trump could do for a man who helped to put him in office, and who refused to testify against the President or take a deal to cook up lies about Russia in order to save his own skin.

It is a tragic irony of Roger Stone's life that a man so closely associated with dirty tricks and the dark arts of politics should, in his private life, be so extraordinarily loyal and moral. These may not be qualities the President himself possesses in abundance, but they are qualities his Appalachian voters cherish.

Beg, plead and cajole as Trump's circle, and the Republican base, might, the President never caved to the pressure to issue Stone a pardon or commutation—despite the near-universal certainty from the Left that Stone would be released from his fate. In other words, it was a pardon that would cost Trump almost nothing politically... yet the President wouldn't do it. As this book went to press, he still hadn't. No one can work out why.

President Trump tweeted, mere minutes after Stone's conviction: "Now they have convicted Roger Stone for lying to Congress and want to give him a long prison term. What about Crooked Hillary, Comey, Strzok, Page, McCabe, Brennan, Clapper, Schiff, Ohr, Steele and Mueller himself all lied and not been prosecuted. This is double standard like never seen before in our country."

And he told Fox News, on Christmas Eve 2019, of his fondness for Stone, that Stone was a "nice guy who many people like." He quickly reiterated that Roger Stone "was a good person" who had been treated "very unfairly." It's time for the President to act on his own words.

Unfortunately, Roger Stone was convicted of lying to Adam Schiff, rather than, say, selling fentanyl. So he'll be ineligible for President Trump's much-lauded First

Step Act. Yet, if there's one person the President surely ought to excuse from a lengthy prison sentence, surely it is Stone.

Pardoning Stone would be another unacknowledged gift to black America, by the way. I can't think of another Republican so ferociously in support of reforming the drug laws, especially on marijuana. Even *The Root* would have to applaud his release given the hours he's put in on weed legalization.

Joking aside, it's the right thing to do. And it might just win back some of the fans, your humble author included, who are wondering if Donald J. Trump has ever, in his entire life, repaid a favor, kept a promise, or stuck by an ally in need.

Trump has done nothing to help, and in some cases has never even publicly acknowledged, his most enthusiastic and effective supporters from the 2016 election as their lives and livelihoods have been destroyed thanks to Silicon Valley censorship and media blacklisting and slander. Not a single banned right-wing celebrity was invited to this year's social media summit at the White House, ostensibly convened to discuss the problem. Trump won't give interviews to any of them or discuss them by name, preferring to retreat to safe endorsements of Turning Point U.S.A., an organization whose leadership grows increasingly out of step with Republican voters and even its own membership, like *National Review* and the Republican Party before it.

No one has suffered more than Stone, but there's a whole army of disgruntled activists, authors and political celebrities behind him whose noses are out of joint. But whatever the financial and professional hardships early and loud Trump supporters have endured, they are as nothing when set against the thuggish dawn raid on Roger Stone's home and his prosecution for alleged gotcha offenses that have nothing to do with Wikileaks or Russia.

They—we—are right to feel aggrieved. But while I can't speak for others, from my point of view, all would be forgiven if the President would just pardon Stone, demonstrating that he is indeed capable of recognizing and rewarding loyalty and taking care of the people who have taken care of him.

Stone did nothing wrong, besides perhaps forgetting about an email one time or another when voluntarily providing help to Congress, and sending a few purple text messages. He's ostentatious, and an expert political strategist with a knack for wrongfooting Democrats, and he is facing a laundry list of alleged process crimes that have nothing to do with Russian collusion, Wikileaks collaboration or anything else of substance. It is easy to see Stone's trial as revenge for Mueller failing to pin anything on Trump. And that's exactly what it is, at least in part.

But, to repeat it one last time, the real reason Stone is being punished by the administrative state to this remarkably vindictive extent is that he refused to betray Trump. Unlike just about everyone else who has ever worked with the President, Roger Stone has stubbornly declined to disavow or lie about President Trump to save himself. This is in keeping with the character of the man I know.

It's a sickening reality of contemporary America that loyalty has become a liability. Public life rewards treachery and deception more than integrity. If you want to get ahead in 2020, telling lies for money in the pages of the *New York Times* or the *Washington Post* is a great way to go.

Roger Stone's trial was a state-orchestrated political assassination; a show trial with a foregone conclusion. Deep-state actors like Department of Justice *éminence grise* Andrew Weissman, cloaking themselves in the legitimacy of a name like Robert Mueller's, had been plotting it all for years. Witnesses for the prosecution included multiple people the government had literally just found guilty of lying, or whose testimony was highly suspect and already contradicted by the President, in writing, to the Special Counsel, by other, highly credible, witnesses in other trial proceedings, by evidence, or by contemporaneous press reports. And the judge was an ass.

I'm not accusing Judge Amy Berman Jackson of acting improperly, of course. I wouldn't dream of it! Except, you know, she clearly did. I see why the government worked so hard to get her. She could not have been more accommodating to their wishes. From her frequent sighs and eye-rolls in court whenever Roger's lawyers were speaking, none of us was left in any doubt about what she thinks of boisterous hellraisers and raconteurs like Roger Stone. And the brazenness of her pronouncements shocked every pew in the gallery.

"Any suggestion that the prosecutors in this case did anything untoward, unethical, or improper is incorrect," Jackson determined in February, perhaps forgetting that she had barred any investigation into precisely that question a few short weeks previously. So, uh, how could anyone know?

A two-year investigation into Russia that cost American taxpayers almost $32 million has produced nothing, even after Special Counsel Robert Mueller threatened to indict people, such as author Jerry Corsi, unless they cook up false testimony to put Roger Stone behind bars and to incriminate the President. Stone's trial turned into a skirmish between a forlorn Stone and a series of proven felonious liars with whom the state had struck deals for testimony in exchange for more lenient sentences. The proven liars with the plea deals prevailed.

Roger Stone denied all of the trivial and vindictive charges levelled at him and passed two polygraphs. Meanwhile, if you were an acquaintance, former employee or intimate of Roger Stone's, you were advised not defend him in public, lest you incurred the wrath of Judge Jackson for saying the wrong thing. The First Amendment didn't apply to friends of Donald Trump: We had to remain silent as Stone's name was sullied and slandered on cable news in the run-up to his trial.

Judge Jackson said of Stone: "He was not prosecuted, as some have complained, for standing up for the President. He was prosecuted for covering up for the President." But this is heinously and obviously wrong.

When Stone attorney Seth Ginsberg spoke for the final time on his client's behalf on February 20, 2020, he described the Roger I knew. "He's devoted himself, for example, to causes that benefit veterans. He also devotes considerable time to the welfare of animals. And he, in that regard, has offered his services, *pro bono*, to a lobbying group that has successfully fought to end certain cruel testing on animals.

"He's also done a great deal of work to assist N.F.L. players who have suffered from traumatic brain injuries. In fact, that work caused a person, the wife of a retired N.F.L. player who doesn't know Mr. Stone, to write to Your Honor and say this man, who has, really, no particular connection to me or my husband or any of these other N.F.L. players who have suffered these horrible injuries, has done such tremendous work that he's had a direct personal impact on our lives."

Ironically, the best description of Stone heard at any point during the trial, from within the courtroom or outside of it, came from Judge Jackson herself, when she described letters she had received about the trial. "Those friends, along with his family, have also painted a portrait of the personal side of Mr. Stone; loving, caring, funny. A good man. Several letters report that when he got married, he treated his stepdaughter and her daughter as his own. Supported them through times of crisis and transition, and through good times as well. The granddaughter, who's now grown, wrote a beautiful letter of her own, attesting to the bond that they share.

"I've learned about the lengths he went to to support his in-laws when they were struggling with the devastating effects of Alzheimer's disease. He has not just been caring and generous within his family. He provided housing and support for an elderly friend who was no longer able to live alone on his boat. He assisted another disabled woman when she was homeless. He's rescued countless dogs and listened and come to the aid of many friends.

"It's consistent with the letters from others who aren't related, who shared friendships even across the political divide, and who have come together with Mr. Stone on issues such as medical marijuana and the strict drug laws that used to apply in New York City.

"He added his voice, his political acumen to important causes such as animal rights, ending inhumane treatment and medical experimentations, same-sex marriage, criminal justice reform, product safety standards, compensation for retired football players with brain injuries, and encouraging the Republican Party to take a hard look at issues facing people of color in America. The letters are compelling and they are sincere."

If all that doesn't persuade you, consider Stone's two most conspicuous critics during the trial, an odious duo embodying the vanishingly few conservatives who had anything negative to say about Trump or Stone:

National Review's Kevin D. Williamson, the man dumb enough to believe that a life in Right-wing punditry could seamlessly translate into a cushy job at the *Atlantic* and who wrote that Stone deserved "a severe punishment" and *Daily Beast* piñata and five-time winner of the most unlikable woman in America award, Meghan McCain, who described Stone as a "bastard from hell who should rot in jail." Next case!

* * *

Roger Stone's is not the only travesty of justice in the Trump era. I have watched as members of the Proud Boys pro-Western fraternity have been sent to jail for the crime of defending themselves against violent attacks from Antifa terrorists—because they would not roll over and just get beaten up. Their trials, too, were engineered into public character assassinations and political spectacles.

Now I am watching my friend Roger face life, and maybe even death, behind bars. He still refuses to countenance the easy, disreputable way out and lie about Trump to strike a deal.

It is heroic, but it is also heartbreaking.

For some of us, who have watched the President struggle to deliver his campaign promises while tossing his allies to the wolves, the Stone case is his ultimate test. It is the moment he can win us back by righting an injustice borne of malice and deep state politicking. It can serve as a precursor to wholesale reform of the sloppy rubric and questionable legal environment that produced the Special Counsel in the first place, protecting future Presidents of either political stripe from the absurd expansionist instincts and waste of resources represented by these boundless, endless legal inquiries.

As Alexis de Tocqueville first observed, America will lose itself if it loses confidence in the justice system and the fairness of trial by jury. Serving on juries and observing the Law being applied without fear or favor is how American citizens come to know justice and the basis for their faith in government.

Citizens of the United States have no King or Queen, no hereditary institution with limitless power, to guarantee the Law. They have only themselves. If the citizens are corrupt—if their service on juries is not honest, as Tomeka Hart's was not honest—it is even worse than voter fraud. Because while voter fraud in elections misrepresents the will of the people, corruption of jury trials destroys the sacred basis of the Law.

I say sacred because there is a reason for God's Commandment against bearing false witness that reveals itself here. Lying under oath, as Tomeka Hart undeniably did, and as Judge Amy Berman Jackson incontestably permitted, is the end of the Law—and thus, ultimately, the end of the American experiment.

Instead of a King, America has a system of rules designed to protect everyone, an elected branch of government to form new strictures and injunctions, an independent judiciary to interpret and apply those injunctions, and an executive to enforce the resolutions judges make. In the absence of a monarch, to safeguard this system and act as a check on injustice or error, the power of clemency and pardon are gifted to duly elected Presidents. It is a power you cannot dispense with in a well-ordered society, even if you dispense with the Crown.

The presidential pardon is a little slice of monarchical oversight hidden inside America's Constitution—a hint, perhaps, that even the Framers did not wholly trust the system of government they were creating. Its inclusion suggests an implied, corollary word of advice to the slippery denizens of the swamp: If you do not want a King, stop abusing the Law.

When something goes wrong—when a citizen lies, violating her oath, or when a judge loses her way, or when, as in this case, both happen in concert—the President is there to remedy it. It is not only in the President's power to grant forgiveness or pardon to the wronged party; it is a moral responsibility, and a core function of his office. It's the whole reason he's elected. All this to say, should it not now be obvious: Do something, Mister President. Do it now.

APPENDIX I: AMENDMENTS

Amendment I

Congress shall make no law respecting an establishment of religion, or prohibiting the free exercise thereof; or abridging the freedom of speech, or of the press; or the right of the people peaceably to assemble, and to petition the Government for a redress of grievances.

Amendment IV

The right of the people to be secure in their persons, houses, papers, and effects, against unreasonable searches and seizures, shall not be violated, and no Warrants shall issue, but upon probable cause, supported by Oath or affirmation, and particularly describing the place to be searched, and the persons or things to be seized.

Amendment V

No person shall be held to answer for a capital, or otherwise infamous crime, unless on a presentment or indictment of a Grand Jury, except in cases arising in the land or naval forces, or in the Militia, when in actual service in time of War or public danger; nor shall any person be subject for the same offence to be twice put in jeopardy of life or limb; nor shall be compelled in any criminal case to be a witness against himself, nor be deprived of life, liberty, or property, without due process of law; nor shall private property be taken for public use, without just compensation.

Amendment VI

In all criminal prosecutions, the accused shall enjoy the right to a speedy and public trial, by an impartial jury of the State and district wherein the crime shall have been committed, which district shall have been previously ascertained by law, and to be informed of the nature and cause of the accusation; to be confronted with the witnesses against him; to have compulsory process for obtaining witnesses in his favor, and to have the Assistance of Counsel for his defence.

APPENDIX II: TESTIMONY

Here is the full text of Roger Stone's September 2017 testimony to the House intelligence committee. The committee would not allow him to testify publicly, but Stone released the text of his opening statement to the media shortly afterward.

Good morning Mr. Chairman, Mr. Ranking Member, Committee members of the House Permanent Select Committee on Intelligence, and staff. My name is Roger J. Stone, Jr., and with me today are my counsel, Grant Smith and Robert Buschel. I am most interested in correcting a number of falsehoods, misstatements, and misimpressions regarding allegations of collusion between Donald Trump, Trump associates, The Trump Campaign and the Russian state. I view this as a political proceeding because a number of members of this Committee have made irresponsible, indisputably, and provably false statements in order to create the impression of collusion with the Russian state without any evidence that would hold up in a US court of law or the court of public opinion.

I am no stranger to the slash and burn aspect of American politics today. I recognize that because of my long reputation and experience as a partisan warrior, I am a suitable scapegoat for those who would seek to persuade the public that there were wicked, international transgressions in the 2016 presidential election. I have a long history in this business: I strategize, I proselytize, I consult, I electioneer, I write, I advocate, and I prognosticate.

I'm a *New York Times* bestselling author, I have a syndicated radio show and a weekly column, and I report for InfoWars.com at 5 o'clock eastern every day. While some may label me a dirty trickster, the members of this Committee could not point to any tactic that is outside the accepted norms of what political strategists and consultants do today. I do not engage in any illegal activities on behalf of my clients or the causes in which I support. There is one "trick" that is not in my bag and that is treason.

As someone whose political activism was born from the anti-communism of Senator Barry Goldwater and President Ronald Reagan; and whose freedom seeking family members were mowed-down by Russian tanks on the streets of Budapest in 1956, I deeply resent any allegation that I would collude with the oppressive Russian state to affect the outcome of the 2016 presidential election.

My colleague, Michael Caputo, voluntarily sat in this seat a couple of months ago, gave what I believe were candid and truthful answers to those who cared to sit in on the interview; and yet, when he was done, he was accused of perjury by a member who did not even have the pretention to show up for his interview. He was eviscerated by some Committee members and consequently, the press. The most unfair aspect of this turn of events, and behavior by some Committee members, is that this Committee refuses, to this day, to release the transcripts of his testimony for the world to read and judge for themselves.

Multiple members of this Committee have made false allegations against me in public session in order to ensure that these bogus charges received maximum media coverage. Now however, you deny me the opportunity to respond to these charges in the same open forum. This is cowardice. Fortunately, we will have the opportunity today to take the exact words of some members of this Committee and examine them in order to uncover the lies.

Members of this Committee as well as some members of the Senate Intelligence Committee aren't alone in their irresponsibility. On January 20, 2017, the *New York Times* reported that the intelligence services were in possession of emails, records of financial transactions and transcripts of telephone intercepts, which proved that Roger Stone, Paul Manafort, and Carter Page colluded with the Russians for the benefit of Donald Trump. So, where are these records? Can this Committee or our intelligence agencies produce them? I didn't think so.

Nor, is this irresponsibility entirely partisan. Sen. John McCain told C.N.N. that I "...should be compelled to appear before the Senate to explain my ties to Yanukovych and the Russians." This is very simple, Senator the answer is: "None" and "None." In fact, I worked against Yanukovych's party in the 2006 parliamentary elections in Ukraine, and have no ties to any Russians.

Given this Committee's consistent refusal to allow me to testify in a public session, in the interest of compromise, I have repeatedly requested that the transcript of my testimony here today, be released immediately upon conclusion of today's session. Even this constructive suggestion has been rejected. What is it you fear? Why do you oppose transparency? What is it you don't want the public to know?

I can assure each of you, I will not let myself be a punching bag for people with ill intentions or political motives. Understand, I will expose the truth in every forum and on every platform available to me.

As a 40-year friend and advisor of Donald Trump, I had continually urged him to run for the presidency, beginning in 1988. When he decided in 2015 to become a serious candidate against a weak slate of opponents, I became one of the Trump campaign's first consultants, reprising a role I played in 2012 when Donald Trump briefly considered a candidacy in that election.

I performed consulting work for the campaign for five months and the consulting relationship ended in August

2015. I, however, didn't go quietly into the night, I continued to work, write, and advocate on behalf of his candidacy because to this day, I believe he has the potential to be a truly transformative President and to make our nation great again.

These hearings are largely based on a yet unproven allegation that the Russian state is responsible for the hacking of the D.N.C. and John Podesta and the transfer of that information to WikiLeaks. No member of this Committee or intelligence agency can prove this assertion. Because the D.N.C. steadfastly refused to allow the F.B.I. to examine their computer servers, this entire claim is based on a self-serving report by CloudStrike, a forensic I.T. company retained by, directed, and paid for by the D.N.C.

The *Nation* magazine recently reported on a study issued by Veteran Intelligence Professionals for Sanity (V.I.P.S.), which is comprised of numerous former high-level U.S. intelligence officials. Based upon the V.I.P.S. study, the *Nation* concluded that, "There was no hack of the Democratic National Committee's system on July 5, 2016... not by the Russians and not by anyone else. Hard science now demonstrates it was a leak- a download executed locally with a memory key or a similarly portable data storage device. In short, they reported it was an inside job by someone with access to the D.N.C.'s system.

This casts serious doubt on the alleged initial "hack," that led to the very consequential publication of a large store of documents on WikiLeaks last summer." Additionally, these unproven allegations have led to a frivolous lawsuit filed by former Obama administration lawyers against me and the Trump campaign. In my motion to dismiss, I submitted a sworn declaration of Dr. Virgil Griffith, a cognitive computer graduate from the California Institute of Technology, who questioned the unproven assumptions that Russian hackers are responsible for theft of D.N.C. emails and other data.

I recognize that those who believe that there was collusion between the Trump camp and the Russian state, now say Stone, "MUST HAVE" been involved, but that is not based on one shred of evidence. This is nothing more than conjecture, supposition, projection, allegation, and coincidence, none of it proven by evidence or fact. I understand the Committee's interest in me, I use all clauses of the 1st Amendment to achieve my goals, I am out there, I am provocative and partisan, but let's be clear, I have no involvement in the alleged activities that are within the publicly stated scope of this Committee's investigation—collusion with the Russian state to affect the outcome of the 2016 election.

I have every right to express my views in the public square. I actively participate in matters of great public concern. I also believe, and you should too, my friend, Tucker Carlson, who said last week, "You should never accept, uncritically, the imprecise conclusions of... the 'intel community.'"

The mantra-like repetition of the claim by our vaunted 17 intelligence agencies that the "Russians" colluded with the Trump campaign to affect the 2016 election, does not make it so. These are, after all, the same entities who insisted the North Koreans would not be able to launch a viable rocket for 3-5 years, that insisted Saddam Hussein was in possession of W.M.D., that there was no torture at Abu Ghraib prison, and that the government had no bulk data collection program, until Edward Snowden revealed otherwise.

Our intelligence agencies have been politicized. I realize they are deeply unhappy over President Trump's refusal to expand the proxy war in Syria and their failure to obtain the no-fly zone promised to them by Hillary Clinton, which would be an open invitation for World War III. That the intelligence agencies have continued to leak, to the detriment of President Trump, in violation of the law, is proof positive of their politicization.

Members of this Committee have made three basic assertions against me which must be rebutted here today. The charge that I knew in advance about, and predicted, the hacking of Clinton campaign chairman John Podesta's email, that I had advanced knowledge of the source or actual content of the WikiLeaks disclosures regarding Hillary Clinton or that, my now public exchange with a persona that our intelligence agencies claim, but cannot prove, is a Russian asset, is anything but innocuous and are entirely false. Again, such assertions are conjecture, supposition, projection, and allegations but none of them are facts.

For example, Mr. Schiff, the ranking member of this Committee asked, "Is it a coincidence that Roger Stone predicted that John Podesta would be a victim of a

Russian hack and have his private emails published, and did so even before Mr. Podesta himself was fully aware that is private emails would be exposed?" I want to know where I predicted this. Can Mr. Schiff read us the exact quote and source from where I predicted the hacking or Mr. Podesta's email? Can Mr. Schiff even come up with a documented quote where I use Podesta and email in the same sentence—before it happened?

My Tweet of August 21, 2016, in which I said, "Trust me, it will soon be the Podesta's time in the barrel. #CrookedHillary" must be examined in context. I posted this at a time that my boyhood friend and colleague, Paul Manafort, had just resigned from the Trump campaign over allegations regarding his business activities in Ukraine. I thought it manifestly unfair that John Podesta not be held to the same standard.

Note, that my Tweet of August 21, 2016, makes no mention, whatsoever, of Mr. Podesta's email, but does accurately predict that the Podesta brothers' business activities in Russia with the oligarchs around Putin, their uranium deal, their bank deal, and their Gazprom deal, would come under public scrutiny. Podesta's activities were later reported by media outlets as diverse as the *Wall Street Journal* and *Bloomberg*. My extensive knowledge of the Podesta brothers' business dealings in Russia was based on the Panama Papers, which were released in early 2016, which revealed that the Podesta brothers had extensive business dealings in Russia.

The Tweet is also based on a comprehensive, early August opposition research briefing provided to me by investigative journalist, Dr. Jerome Corsi, which I then asked him to memorialize in a memo that he sent me on August 31st, all of which was culled from public records. There was no need to have John Podesta's email to learn that he and his presidential candidate were in bed with the clique around Putin. In fact, FactCheck.org, a news organization funded by the Annenberg Foundation, reported, "There is nothing in the public record so far that proves Stone, a political operative and longtime Trump associate, predicted the Podesta email hack."

Now, let me address the charge that I had advance knowledge of the timing, content and source of the WikiLeaks disclosures from the D.N.C. On June 12, 2016, WikiLeaks' publisher Julian Assange, announced that he was in possession of Clinton D.N.C. emails. I learned this by reading it on Twitter. I asked a journalist who I knew had interviewed Assange to independently confirm this report, and he subsequently did. This journalist assured me that WikiLeaks would release this information in October and continued to assure me of this throughout the balance of August and all of September. This information proved to be correct. I have referred publicly to this journalist as an, "intermediary", "go-between" and "mutual friend." All of these monikers are equally true.

In the March 20 public session of this Committee, Mr. Schiff asked former F.B.I. Director Comey, "Are you aware that Mr. Stone also stated publicly that he was in direct communication with Julian Assange and WikiLeaks?" The way the question was asked was clearly designed to cast me in a bad light. I have never said or written that I had any direct communication with Julian Assange and have always clarified in numerous interviews and speeches that my communication with WikiLeaks was through the aforementioned journalist. Again, Mr. Schiff is guilty of a false assertion.

The fact is that during the March 20 Comey hearing and many times subsequent, members of this Committee, and even Democratic nominee for President, felt that they could go into the public square and make similar charges without any substantiation or basis in fact.

Congressman Heck of Washington, stated, for example, "... we've heard about quite a few individuals in the Trump orbit who fell somewhere on that spectrum from mere naïveté, disturbing enough if this naïveté is a feature of those (who) were supposed to be running our country and foreign policy, to unwitting Russian dupes, to willing blindness, to active coordination. This rogues gallery includes those already fired- Roger Stone, adviser to Donald Trump..."

This is the worst sort of neo-McCarthyism. To be clear, I have never represented any Russian clients, have never been to Russia, and never had any communication with any Russians or individuals fronting for Russians, in connection with the 2016 presidential election.

To pile on, in an interview on M.S.N.B.C. on May 19, 2017, Congresswoman Speier felt compelled to say: "I believe that Michael Caputo is part of this cabal including Roger Stone and Paul Manafort, and others who had business relationships with Russia." No, I do not have and I've never had any relationship with Russia or any Russian entity. You have falsely accused me without any evidence – you should apologize today.

One more apology I would demand in public, if she were here today, is from presidential runner-up, Hillary Clinton. Following the lead of the minority members of this Committee, in her new fiction book, she repeats the same false narratives about me as if they were the truth...they could not be further from the truth.

And then there is Congressmen Eric Swalwell who, as reported in *Newsmax*, said, "From Roger Stone, we hope to learn the same things we learned from Paul Manafort, Carter Page, Don [Trump] Jr., and others who were particularly active in their dealings with Russians during the summer of 2016." Has Mr. Swalwell read my exchange with the Twitter persona which he alleges constitutes collusion? The exchange is innocuous at best. Since I had no other contact with Russians, what could he be referring to?

Finally, let me address this limited, benign, and now entirely public exchange with a persona on Twitter calling themselves Guccifer 2.0. While some in the intelligence community have claimed that Guccifer 2.0 is a Russian cutout and that it is responsible for the hacking of the D.N.C. servers, neither of these assertions can be proven by this Committee or the aforementioned intelligence community. I wrote an article for *Breitbart* on August 5, 2016, in which I express my view that Guccifer 2.0 was not a Russian asset, at the same time reporting their claim taking credit for hacking the D.N.C..

My only exchange with Guccifer 2.0 would begin on August 14, 2016, after my article appeared, and ran through September 9, 2016. Imagine my deep when Mr. Schiff purposefully conflated these dates before this Committee, reversing them to create the false impression that I had communicated with Guccifer 2.0 on Twitter prior to publication of the article questioning whether Guccifer 2.0 is a Russian cut-out. Shame on you Mr. Schiff.

Now that more information is in the public domain, the very question of whether Guccifer 2.0 hacked the D.N.C. must be revisited in light of the V.I.P.S. report cited by *The Nation*. As they concluded, "Forensic investigations of documents made public two weeks prior to the July 5 leak by the person or entity known as Guccifer 2.0 show that they were fraudulent: Before Guccifer posted them they were adulterated by cutting and pasting them into a blank template that had Russian as its default language.

Guccifer took responsibility on June 15 for an intrusion the D.N.C. reported on June 14 and professed to be a WikiLeaks source—claims essential to the official narrative implicating Russia in what was soon cast as an extensive hacking operation. To put the point simply, forensic science now devastates this narrative." I am left to conclude that the President is right when he calls this Congressional investigation a, "witch hunt."

Based on what we know now, it is clear that there was a foreign nation which was colluding with a presidential campaign in an attempt to influence the outcome of the

2016 presidential election. Therefore, I strongly urge this Committee to investigate the numerous, publicly documented contacts between Ukraine and the Clinton campaign, particularly in light of recent public reports that Ukraine is now providing sophisticated missile technology to North Korea. Please do not continue to perpetuate falsehoods here today.

A portion of the proceeds from this book will be donated to the Roger Stone Legal Defense Fund.

Readers can contribute at stonedefensefund.com

ABOUT THE AUTHOR

Milo Yiannopoulos is an award-winning journalist, a *New York Times*-bestselling author, an international political celebrity, America's original and best-known free speech martyr, a comedian, an accomplished entrepreneur, a hair icon, a penitent and, to the annoyance of his many enemies, an exceedingly happy person. He is the most censored, most lied-about man in the world, banned from stepping foot on entire continents for his unapologetic commitment to free expression. But he is also, somehow, one of the most sought-after speakers anywhere, invited by foreign governments, wealthy individuals and even the occasional courageous private company to share his unique blend of laughter and war. Milo lurches from improbable triumph to improbable triumph, loathed by establishment Left and Right alike. His first book, *Dangerous*, sold over 200,000 copies, despite never being reviewed in any major publication. Milo lives in New Jersey with his husband, John.

CPSIA information can be obtained
at www.ICGtesting.com
Printed in the USA
BVHW081018150320
575060BV00001B/247